Themes and Projects in Art and Design

Above *Resources assembled for a project. Jan Reeves. 1987*

Themes and Projects in Art and Design

Frederick Palmer

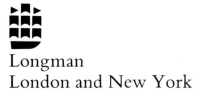

Longman
London and New York

Longman Group UK Limited,
Longman House, Burnt Mill, Harlow,
Essex CM20 2JE, England
and Associated Companies throughout the world.

Published in the United States of America
by Longman Inc., New York.

First published 1988
Second impression 1989

ISBN 0–582–35591–5

Produced by Longman Group (FE) Ltd
Printed in Hong Kong

British Library Cataloguing in Publication Data

Palmer, Frederick, 1936–
    Themes and projects in art and design.
    1. Art — Study and teaching (Elementary)
    I. Title
    707'.1   N350

    ISBN 0–582–35591–5

Library of Congress Cataloging in Publication Data

Palmer, Frederick, 1936–
    Themes and projects in art and design.

    Bibliography: p.
    Includes index.
    1. Art — Study and teaching (Secondary) 2. Project
method in teaching.   I. Title.
N350.P263   1988   700   87–2789
ISBN 0–582–35591–5

Cover photograph: Iznik tiles, from the portico facade
of the Rüstem Pasa Mosque, Istanbul. Sinan (mid 16th
century). Photograph by Dr Ahmet Ertug/Zamana
Gallery, London.

Contents

To all teachers of art and design (especially those
'south of the river').

'I will suggest the waterfront more than cover it ...'

Thomas Mallon
1984

Acknowledgements

We are grateful to the museums and galleries acknowledged in the captions for permission to reproduce photographs, and also to the following;

Allen, Brady and Marsh, page 123; Arts Council, page 17 (photo Carl Gabriel Cocoyea); Batsford, Frederick Palmer, *Visual Awareness*, page 97; Columbia-EMI-Warner, page 104 below; *Coventry Evening Telegraph*, page 73 below; Diamond Information Centre/ J. Walter Thompson Company, pages 16–17; Format Photographers, page 19 right (photo Jenny Matthews); Sonia Halliday and Laura Lushington/Dean and Chapter of Canterbury Cathedral, page 22; Kobal Collection/Warner Brothers, page 39 below; Lauros/ Giraudon, page 105 above; Longman Photographic Unit, page 29 right; Longman 1984, page 85 above; Michelin Tyre Company, page 115; Mumbles Railway Publishing/Ribble Motor Services, page 87 above left; *The Picture Magazine*, 1893, page 55 below, 60 above right, 64 above, 80 below left, 132 below, 141 below and 143 above; George Rodger, 1980/Acme Cards, London, page 66; Science Photo Library, page 118 (photo David Parker); Shell Photographic Service, page 60 left; Singer Consumer Products, page 130; TI Creda, page 64 below; Toyota/SSC & B:Lintas, page 138; Werner Forman Archive, pages 41 centre right and 101 below; World of Islam Festival Publishing Company, Issam El-Said and Ayse Parman, *Geometric Concepts in Islamic Art*, 1976, pages 110, 121 below left and below right. The writing of this book has relied on the goodwill and encouragement of a number of people. Those galleries, museums and individuals who have kindly allowed me to reproduce works from their collections should be thanked for their cooperation. In this category I am particularly grateful to Jane De ' Athe, Director of the Zamana Gallery, London; Jake Barker of DMB & B; Laurence Carey of H & P Associates; Alistair Duncan, Director of the World of Islam Festival Trust; Bob Godfrey, the film-maker; Barbara Heller for the tapestries from the Wissa Wassef Art School, Cairo; John Sheeran, Curator of the Bradford City Art Gallery and Giles Waterfield, Director of the Dulwich Picture Gallery.

In addition there are those friends and colleagues who have been especially generous with both their comments and time. I am extremely grateful to the following: Fanny Baldwin, who has given me throughout the benefit of her enthusiasm and educational experience, Norman Binch for writing the Introduction and for his constructive advice and support, Joe Connolly for commenting on parts of the manuscript, Charles Salter for continual debate and discussion on the examination, my son Jake for taking and printing many of the photographs and my wife Eunice for her continual forebearance.

Frederick Palmer
1988

Introduction

This book by Frederick Palmer is a timely addition to several recent books on art and design education. Understandably, they are all mainly concerned with secondary education, which is now subject to the greatest single influence that most of us have experienced in our professional lives.

That influence is, of course, the GCSE examination. Art and design, in common with most other school subjects, is now subject to agreed National Criteria which, in the broadest interpretation, represents a consensus of opinion on what it should be about. For many teachers this is a loss of freedom which threatens their professional integrity, and yet the outcome seems to be that, within the obvious constraints, there is enormous opportunity to develop new courses and new kinds of art and design education. In fact, the General Criteria, which govern the whole examination, specifically encourage curriculum development and new ways of learning.

The most significant aspects of the new examination for art and design, are the emphases given to 'active learning', 'resource-based learning', and 'self-directed study'. The guide published by the Open University for the Secondary Examinations Council, explains these terms in some detail. However, most teachers need support in trying to understand the implications, and in developing appropriate course content and teaching/learning strategies. This book will help to do just that.

Perhaps the greatest innovation is the requirement to teach art and design in its social, cultural and historical context. In fact the syllabus includes political and economic considerations in the list, but for most practical purposes, it can simply be thought of as teaching and learning in an appropriate context. There have been strong pressures to extend the teaching of the history of art and design for many years, but the constrained circumstances in which most art teachers work, and have been trained, do not allow much new content to be included. Now that it is rapidly becoming an obligation to give proper consideration to contextual studies, the main difficulty is in knowing what to do and how.

The examples provided in this book, combine practical work with theoretical and contextual studies, and should provide a most valuable means of exploring the new system. What they most seek to encourage is the development of more independent learning on the part of the student, within the safety of carefully constructed programmes of work.

It is not prescriptive and I hope that it will help and encourage teachers to develop their own ideas in similar ways.

Norman Binch

The images in this book are not subsidiary to the text. Many are more than illustrations of the words, making singly and in conjunction one with another, additional points; acting as suggestions for project work just as much as the written material does.

In most cases they have been selected from collections in London and provincial galleries and museums so that some, if not all, will be available for first hand experience by the students. Furthermore, where possible lesser known works have been reproduced, not to supplant the more familiar and perhaps greater, but in order to broaden the experience.

The areas of study listed under each project are simply aspects of the theme which will allow the student to work at his or her own level. They are not detailed accounts of the subject nor are they lists of practical activities, but each is a basis for personal research and interpretation. The practical work, the media used and decisions about procedure should be the result of discussion between student and teacher.

Below Gertrude Bell, Daughter of the Desert. *Joanna Buxton. Tapestry. Courtesy of the artist. (See pages 23 and 26.) Some works from private collections have been reproduced in this book in order to add an element of the unfamiliar and also to indicate areas for consideration rather than particular images for study*

Project–Based Learning

Top Screw mobile. *Kenneth Martin.*
Copper and bronze. (See pages 127 and
135.)
Above *Isphahan diagrams (see page 121).*

The aim of this book is to provide teachers of art and design with a selection of themes for projects which they may develop, in ways which are appropriate to the needs of their students, in the light of the General Certificate of Secondary Education. It is not a book about the examination, nor is it a comprehensive guide to course planning. It should, perhaps, also be clearly stated that the readers for whom this book is intended are qualified teachers conversant with both the broad, general concepts of education as well as with the specific issues dealt with in the national and regional documents produced for the new examination. This publication is therefore not a textbook of educational theory. What are presented are starting points open to many interpretations; indications of possible directions which may help the teacher organise variations on project themes for group and individual learning. Decisions about the media to be used will have to be made by students and teachers, as will the selection of working methods, for these are dependent upon circumstance and not the direction of a writer unfamiliar with individual requirements. This, then, is not a book of recipes for successful practice. It contains not prescriptions, but suggestions which, pointing the way to investigation and discovery, may promote ideas and indicate areas of study across the curriculum.

Although project-based learning is only one of many ways of working in art and design, it can be an amalgam of a number of learning procedures. Within the context of a project there may be emphasis on the acquisition of a skill, the learning of a practice, visual analysis, critical analysis, problem solving or expressive interpretation. Such procedures may, of course, be employed singly or in conjunction one with another.

Reasons for the selection of any working procedure should, where possible, be appreciated by the student and its appropriateness to the work being undertaken ought to be fully understood. Whereas the experienced teacher will know the procedures relevant to the individual student and those most sensible for the work being done, it is of course desirable for the student to be involved in the selection. The decision to adopt one particular method at the beginning of a course of work does not preclude a combination with others as the work progresses. The most obvious example of this is the inclusion at most stages of discussion and critical appraisal of both the work and the method. That is, process analysis integrated with whatever visual research and working procedure has been adopted.

A great deal of emphasis has been placed, in the recent past, on the acquisition of skill and the importance of working from observation.

Although these are essential parts of the art and design curriculum they are not, by any means, the only factors. Personal experience, so strongly emphasised in the GCSE criteria, is not a limitation, but a sound basis for creative work. It should be appreciated though that personal experience is not just about recording accurately the environment and objects in it, but is about the life and interests of the student outside, as well as within, the school. Furthermore, it must also be about responding to, and learning to appraise, the work of contemporary artists, craftsmen, designers and architects as well as those from cultures, countries and times other than our own.

The project themes given in this book have been selected to represent different aspects of the work undertaken by art and design departments. They are, of course, only a limited selection and many other topics would fit into the thematic groupings given here. The first three, *portraits, environment* and *interiors* are familiar subject-based themes dealing with people and places. *Advertising* and *celebration* allow for the exploration of social processes and events, both of which have powerful public and private influences on our lives. Art and design practices themselves may also be starting points, although it will probably be wise to take some aspect rather than attempting a full survey. *Drawing* has been selected as representative of a practice common to all areas of art and design. Painting, modelling, weaving or any other practice could equally well have been chosen. *Pattern and texture* and *structure* represent two formal properties which are present in a work of art and have been selected because they are elements of both two and three-dimensional work; line and colour would be obvious alternative choices or combinations. *Movement and time* and *series, serial and sequence* are examples of more abstract and conceptual themes. Both relate to the study of mass media and popular culture, and also to the exploration of the relationships between the visual and performing arts; drama, music and dance.

One of the main considerations of the GCSE is for an art and design curriculum somewhat broader in scope than has been the case previously. It is for an expansion from the concentration on the Western European fine art tradition which has been the mainstay of art in schools for so long; the encouragement of graphic and constructional design; the forging of cross-cultural and curricular links and the fostering of a greater element of student participation. These considerations should be constantly in the mind of the teacher planning art and design courses.

The 'guide for teachers' produced by the Secondary Examinations Council in collaboration with the Open University, lists three areas which are important considerations in terms of curriculum development. These are: active learning, resource-based learning and equal opportunities.

Active learning is student centred; may be student initiated and is concerned with the student taking responsibility. It is learning by doing, which means researching as well as making, and is therefore resource-based. Active learning, as opposed to the passive reception of factual information, is what most art and design education has always been about and in order to maximise the effectiveness of such a method the best departments have made available a wide and stimulating selection of reference and resource material. Resources, however, are more than a few empty wine bottles, crushed soft drink cans, crumpled crisp packets, odd baseball boots and dusty plants. These items, seen so often in art rooms in the recent past, are

Top *Sequence from a Kleenex television advertisement. Courtesy of DMB & B. (See page 56.)*

Above *Michelin advertising series. (See page 115.)*

10

Top Mask of Rangda, Widow Witch, Goddess of Evil Spirits. Bali. 1985. (See page 74.)

Above Chahkobi tea serving doll without costume. Courtesy of The Japan Foundation. (See pages 127 and 135.)

no longer sufficient for the requirements of the new examinations, nor are they enough to encourage the student and allow for a serious art and design education.

Resource-based learning is an essential part of the GCSE in art and design and consideration should be given to how best we may encourage the students to select and contribute resources for the work in hand. These last two points are particularly important. Surely it is better to involve the student when possible so that the selection of resources is a part of their creative experience, not always a collection of objects imposed by the teacher. Students may not always be willing or able to contribute, but that is no reason for not offering the opportunity, for not encouraging participation, and including resource finding and decision making as a definite part of a project; perhaps as an element of homework.

The considered relationship of the resources to the project in hand is obviously imperative and the finding and selecting of appropriate material will naturally require effort on the part of all concerned. In some cases the art room may need radical alteration, being changed into a different environment with corners of other interiors re-created: gardens, beach scenes or hedge-rows invented; still-life groups arranged to allow for the exploration of selected objects, colour keys, patterns and textures, or the comparison between natural and man-made forms. At other times simpler resources may be required magnifying glasses, for the examination of seed pods, flower heads, dead insects, fossils, shells, watch mechanisms and other miniature objects. What is important is that the art room is a visually stimulating environment, forever changing, flexible in its layout, exciting in its presentation of ideas and materials, always alive and a constant source of wonder.

The resources should change before familiarity creates boredom, the furniture should be moved to accommodate a particular project or series of sessions, and students should have access to back-up material in the form of books, magazines, slides, videos, films, displays of reproductions, photographs and postcards. These should not be considered as extras, but as essentials allowing the student to obtain information related to the practical work and also enabling extensions into the areas of critical and historical studies. Such supporting resources for a project need not always be taken from the world of art and design, although a basic library of such material is essential, but may include images and information from local firms, shops, estate and travel agents, garden centres, supermarkets, building and decorating contractors, and the manufacturing industry. The involvement of people from such agencies may enable positive links to be made with the world of work. Similarly, the community, local services, sport, entertainment and leisure organisations will all contribute, either with materials and information, or personal participation.

Resources for art and design are not limited to the narrow, obviously subject-based areas which are immediately apparent, but are almost infinite; particularly if we are concerned with the broad aspects of education. Natural phenomena in all forms are our traditional subjects for image making, but everything that is 'man-made' begins on the drawing board and so all areas of natural and human activity are our province. We should make use of them if we are to fulfill our role as educators.

In addition, the resources which some departments have made available to students have included gallery and museum visits with perhaps a contribution from the educational staff of those establishments. Project-based learning is by its very nature concerned with these aspects of education. It is about learning by doing rather than by receiving information from the teacher. It is about using resources to elicit a response and to aid research into a chosen topic. It is also a process which can deal with the third point raised, that of equal opportunities in both race and gender. Any research undertaken in a truly broad sense and with a serious attempt to view a theme in the light of historical, political, social and cultural setting must perforce look at the issues of race and gender at some point. This is not to force current interests and policies into the art and design curriculum, but rather to realise that these issues have always been present and that to ignore them is to limit the education of the student to the preconceptions of the past which are, perhaps, not wholly applicable to the contemporary scene, or relevant to the interests and concerns of the young people in society today.

The GCSE examination aims to place greater emphasis on the application of knowledge rather than the mere acquisition of skill or facts and it is therefore imperative that the student is genuinely involved at all stages. This means that there should be an understanding of the work being undertaken, its educational value and the working methods appropriate, and also an analysis of problems and information, an application of skills, a synthesis of ideas and an evaluation of process as well as of the result.

Fuller understanding of the educational aspects of art and design by the student will be aided by the teacher's willingness to make links between what is done in school and the life of the student outside. Mass media, popular culture in all its forms, hobbies and leisure activities are all areas which allow the teacher to make contact and gain some initial commitment which may be built upon. This is not to down-grade the educational components of the course, but to make relevant connections. Similarly, those aspects of the subject which relate to functional applications, that is to design, might also be considered in a similar way, not just as ends in themselves or a design process, but as a practical way of relating what is being learned in school to the current interests and future life of the student. The ability to make informed judgements about the design of our environment and the goods we buy, rather than rely on emotional responses or financial considerations, may enable us not only to select that which satisfies most, but might help to give us a voice in the making of some of those decisions which affect us and which are often made without our being consulted. How can a visually illiterate society expect a visually pleasing environment? The making of serious critical appraisal is not the perogative of the few. It is the concern of us all. Nor is it simply a matter of taste. It is a matter of education. A visual education is as vital to the spiritual growth of the individual, and to a society, as literacy and numeracy.

Education, to be effective, relies on the involvement and commitment of the student; the degree to which the student is motivated. Self-motivated learning, based on the student's interests and requirements implies student involvement in course planning. By the end of the GCSE course the student should be helping to structure the course in a manner which allows for independent research and the development of ideas as they arise and not simply as they have been forseen by the teacher. It goes without saying that there should also be evidence of the student's personal response to the idea or project

Top Fantasie sur le costume moderne. *Leon Baxst. 1912. Whereabouts unknown. (See page 84.)*

Above Omina. *Designer Vernon Williams. Genesis. Notting Hill Carnival Queen 1985. (See page 79.)*

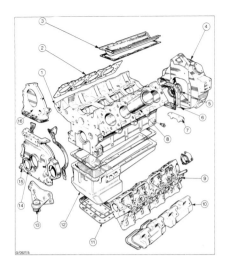

Top *Exploded drawing. Pen and ink. (See page 83.)*

Above *Frontispiece from a Mamluk Koran. Eygpt. Fourteenth century. British Library. (See page 99.)*

theme; as there should be shown in the works produced an understanding of the basic elements of art and design and the media employed. Furthermore, there ought to be interwoven with these, some signs that the student has realised why projects, or other works, have been undertaken; and, certainly of equal importance, how working methods have been used.

The more advanced and committed student might produce work in a wide variety of media, or a deeper study of one medium if the examination is of the endorsed kind; and be conversant with the historical and critical context of the work researched and produced. The wider cultural and cross-curricular relationships will be apparant not only in the visual work but in written forms, in notebooks and research material, as well as in the student's ability to discuss and debate links, influences and implications. In other words, whilst it will be possible for the less able student to work within the structure of the project, responding to the theme and achieving however limited a realisation of an idea from first thought to a final resolution, it will further be possible for the more able student to take the work to whatever level desired and to place it within the broader educational and cultural context. Project-based learning may be either a group or an individual activity, but with intelligent guidance from the teacher it will enable students to work at different levels and to identify ideas and requirements, and realise them to a greater or lesser degree.

How, then, do we assess such work, produced not from setting a given task or problem, but from the student's own concerns, interests and interpretations, thereby deciding personal aims and objectives?

Some understanding of, and sympathy with, those aims and objectives is a necessity, as is a continual involvement throughout the research and creation period; an involvement by the teacher, not an interference. There is much to be said in such a system for the teacher as instigator and then as guide and mentor rather than director. There is certainly a great deal to be said in favour of the teacher who is flexible enough to adapt not only ways of working, but ways of assessing to meet the different needs of different students; and to appreciate that both students and their needs vary from time to time. Such an ability, along with the willingness to constantly question both ways of working and methods of assessment, is necessary if the teacher is not to inflict on the student the limitations of a fixed method and perhaps the problems of a personal prejudice.

There is no simple answer to the question of how we assess art and design. What method or combination of methods is employed is, as every teacher knows, dependent upon the situation and must be appropriate to both the course and the students. Can external assessment ever do this? To what extent the assessment might be negotiated is a matter for the individuals to decide, but that there should be some element of negotiated assessment is obviously desirable given the requirements of the GCSE. How else will it be credible, or even possible, to formulate opinion without an understanding of what was intended, and the context and situation in which the work was produced? Internal assessment by the school supposes an appreciation of the processes undergone as well as the product produced, an awareness of the growth of a student and the knowledge gained rather than the reaction to a selected evidence of skill.

For the first time in this country there are national criteria for the marking of art and design to which teacher and student must refer and which will form the basis of any discussion with external moderators. Assessment is therefore no longer something which happens at the end of a course of study, but a continuous process which is irrevocably tied in with the course work at all stages. The requirements of the examination are related to that course and not solely to a final examination. Some type of continuous assessment is inevitable. The form that takes is dependent upon the nature of the work being undertaken and the course being followed. That course must likewise be shaped by the forms of assessment decided upon. Both are inter-related. Teachers will have to ask themselves continually what form or forms of assessment are appropriate at any given time. Throughout the student's time in school, and certainly during the two years just prior to the examination, a combination of assessment procedures will probably be required: negotiated assessment, teacher assessment, parental assessment and self-assessment, and the student will participate in group discussions and individual tutorials about current work and progress. The extent to which course planning is governed by the methods used and vice versa must surely be a consideration constantly in mind.

Although not by any means the only way of working, project-based learning allows for considerable flexibility in course planning, working methods and assessment procedure and, perhaps more importantly, for serious student involvement at all stages.

Below Little Nemo in Slumberland. *Windsor McCay. 29 October 1905. (See pages 119 and 124.)*

Some Considerations for Modular Courses

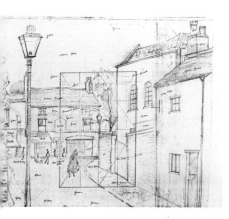

Top *Sketchbook drawing for a painting. Edgar Blakeney. c. 1954. Pencil on paper with pen colour notes. 33.0 × 25.4 cm. (See page 83.)*

Above *The Boatbuilders' Yard, Cookham. Stanley Spencer. City Art Gallery, Manchester*

A structured programe in which there are identifiable goals, understood objectives and stages which allow for a sense of achievement, will encourage student participation and creative involvement more than unconnected tasks set at the start of each lesson.

The following lists some of the considerations which will be part of any project programme. It will be seen that an eight or ten week modular course could easily be based on these.

Teacher

- Discusses with students the project theme, the reasons for its selection, its relevance to the students' life and education.
- Explains the aims of the project.
- Discusses the educational objectives of the project.
- Some students will be able to choose their own objectives based on their interests within the general aim. With experienced students the project theme, as well as its aims and objectives, might be negotiated.

Student

Identifies interest and in consultation with the teacher:
- Decides research.
  1 Primary source material i.e. actual objects and locations.
  2 Relevant secondary source material e.g. photographs, reproductions, books, slides, tapes and videos. These are selected to:
    a assist practical work;
    b place the theme in context;
    c show previous interpretations or solutions by artists, designers and craftpersons.
- Decides suitable working methods.
- Selects appropriate materials and media.
- Works from primary source material to collect information by observation and analysis. This might include recording in a number of ways e.g. drawing, colour notation, photography, film.
- Develops practical work i.e. synthesis of research and ideas.
- Considers possible extensions into other practices and subject areas.
- Evaluates both process and product (after continuous personal assessment and discussion with student colleagues and teacher) in relationship to the original aims and objectives. This might be extended to include other personnel. For example, technicians,

teachers of other subjects, visiting speakers and artists, and the curators and education staff of galleries and museums.

As well as the drawing, painting, designing and constructing skills which working on a project course allows, the student should experience and acquire some of the following:

- perceptual skills;
- research skills;
- conceptual skills;
- interpretative skills (including technical skills);
- communication skills;
- critical skills;
- evaluative skills;

and in so doing learn how, why and when to apply them.

It could be argued that there is a major thematic area missing from the list of projects in this book and that is the area which encompasses the emotions, feelings, the unknown, and consequently many of the issues and concerns which are so close to the young person.

Such themes are not as popular in art departments as they once were. The current vogue for working from direct observation and experience does not favour the expressive response and the concentration on imagination which was used, and some would say abused, a few years ago. Nonetheless, themes such as: dreams, freedom and oppression, fear, good and evil, love and hate, the unknown and the unconscious are of interest to many young people. There is a desire to explore personal feelings and emotions and study the expression of such topics by other artists. It is for this reason that the theme of joy and sorrow has been selected for a more detailed breakdown of a modular course. It should be remembered that the suggestion given below is an example of a course not an exemplar, the details would vary according to the needs of the group and its interests, along with the knowledge and concerns of the teacher.

Theme: joy and sorrow

Aim

To produce a representational painting which expresses joy or sorrow.

Objectives

- To learn something of how colour can evoke emotion in the spectator.
- To understand how the simple pictorial organisation of a painting can affect the spectator's response.
- To appreciate how these two elements of colour and composition have been used by some painters to express feelings of joy and sorrow.
- To realise that these are only two aspects to be considered when attempting to express emotion visually, or when analysing the work of artists.

Discussion

- Reasons for **a** the choice of theme e.g. both are basic human experiences common to us all, and **b** the aim and objectives listed above.
- Discussion on the meaning of the words and their relationship to other similar words e.g. happiness, contentment, sadness, despair.
- Discussion on those images and experiences which make for individual feelings of joy and sorrow and also those wider, more common issues which seem to affect everyone.
- Discussion about visual cliché and stereotypes related to the theme.
- Consideration of two still-life groups set up in advance by the teacher with or without student participation. These would obviously be composed of objects and colours associated with the theme.

Primary source material

Expressive response to the subject i.e. one of the still-life groups chosen by the individual. Followed by discussion of the work produced/museum visit.

Secondary material

Analysis of work by artists from reproductions assembled by the teacher and collected by the students. This would presumably take account of images from the mass media, three-dimensional constructions and other visual sources as well as painting. These might include:

Joy

- Paintings of the Nativity.
- Moghul miniatures.
- Persian miniatures.
- Books of Hours.
- Breugel's paintings of childrens' games, peasant dances and weddings.
- Poussin's paintings of Bacchanalia as well as those by Rubens and Titian.
- Goya's fairground and dance scenes.
- Impressionist paintings of dances, picnics and 14th July Celebrations.
- Paintings of music and dance by Henri Matisse.
- Images of carnivals and celebrations.
- Photographs of current events e.g. sports triumphs, births, weddings, arrivals, first communions, baptisms, barmitzvah, 'Eid al Fitr and 'Eid al-Adha.

Sorrow

- Paintings of crucifixion, *pietà*, martyrdom.
- Images of hell by painters such as Hieronymus Bosch, Pieter Brueghel the Elder.
- Goya's *Disasters of War*.
- Early drawings by Van Gogh.

Above *Notting Hill carnival*

Below *Diamond advertisement*

Above The Mystic Nativity. *Sandro Botticelli. c. 1500. Oil on canvas. 108.6 × 74.9 cm. National Gallery, London*

Top left The Crucifixion. *Attributed to Kesu Das. Mughal c. 1590. Opaque watercolour on paper. 29.5 × 17.8 cm. British Museum, London*

Bottom left Venus Mourning Adonis. *Peter Paul Rubens. c. 1614. Oil on wood panel. 48.5 × 66.5 cm. Dulwich Picture Gallery, London*

Right *An injured child recovering in Quelimane Hospital, Zambezia, Mozambique. December 1986*

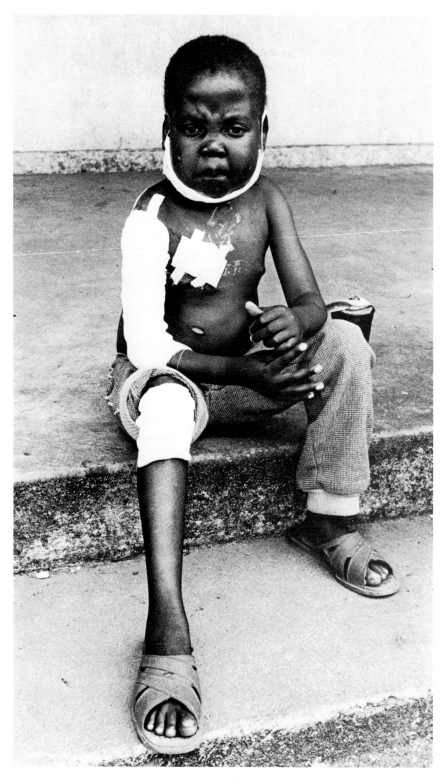

- The engravings of Gustave Doré.
- Picasso's Blue Period works as well as his *Guernica* and *Weeping Woman* series.
- Some of the paintings of Francis Bacon.
- Photographs from various wars and also current disputes e.g. South Africa, Nicaragua, as well as images of famine and deprivation. Advertisements for famine relief, Oxfam, Dr Barnado's, NSPCC, RSPCA. Family photographs commemorating departures and funerals.

It would also be worth considering in this context those images which are of a less obviously representational character but which seek to express emotion in more abstract terms. For example; work by Kandinsky, Klee, Hodgkin as well as Symbolism, Surrealism and Expressionism in general. Sculpture, textiles (such as tapestry), graphic design, theatre, cinema and television could also contribute to work on this theme.

A study of colour and compositional theories related to the theme might be undertaken at this stage.

For example:

RESPONSES TO COLOUR

'Everyone knows that yellow, orange and red suggest ideas of "Joy and plenty"'

DELACROIX

Apart from being able to indicate spatial relationships, colour also gives the spectator a variety of sensations. The fact that certain sections of the colour circle are labelled warm and cool is evidence of this with the associations of sunlight and fire on the one hand and sea and shadow on the other. Consequently people use colour to express their moods and ideas, decorating their homes in particular ways and dressing in a manner which is in keeping with how they feel on a particular day. The warmer colours usually suggest lively, happy feelings whilst the cooler ones are calmer.

Colours are therefore associated with different events and the arousal of different emotions. This is partly due to the nature of the colour itself but also to the role which has been assigned to it by a particular society. Red is traditionally connected with love and passion and gaiety but it is also an international road signal for stop. A fact which apparently annoyed certain of the Red Guard in Communist China during the Cultural Revolution of the sixties who thought that the colour symbolising Communism should not also be used as the symbol for 'Stop'. Numerous cultures have placed a great deal of emphasis on symbolic colours, for instance the ancient Egyptians believed that the colours in dreams were indicative of a whole range of emotions and portents from the white of home happiness through the red of ardent love, the dark blue of success, the light green of a bad omen to the black of death.

The Greek physician Galen, whose ideas persisted into the Middle Ages, wrote about the 'four humours' and their relationship with illness, the elements and colour.*

Humour	Colour	Element
Sanguine	Red (blood)	Air
Choleric	Yellow (gall)	Fire
Melancholic	White (phlegm)	Water

Colour and the elements have been linked in different ways throughout history.

Yellow or Red – Fire
White   – Air, Water or Earth
Black   – Elements in 'transmutation'   *Aristotelian School*

* Galen's Commentary on Hippocrates' *De humoribus* in Karl Gottlob Kuhn (ed), *Claudii Galeni opera omnia XVI*, Leipzig 1829: 'Alberti's Colour Theory' by Samuel Y. Edgerton Jr, *Journal of the Warburg and Courtauld Institute*, Vol XXXII, 1969.

Red – Fire   Green – Water
Blue – Air   Grey – Earth   *Leon Battista Alberti*

In the Middle Ages and the Renaissance colour was not only equated with the elements, but with aspects of astronomy, alchemy, the emotions and religious attributes.

Red – Charity   White – Purity
Yellow-Gold – Dignity Black – Humility   *St Antoninus*

In Western European art the Madonna is usually dressed in blue robes, a colour symbolising happiness and calm; and Christian hope is signified by yellow. In Oriental art Krishna is given blue skin so that the spectator is in no doubt which is the figure of the god.

Certain North American Indian tribes assigned colours to the points of the compass and used them as directional signs as well as ways of predicting the future. Contemporary Western art, however, rarely uses the idea of symbolic colours, relying more on the physical properties and our responses to them rather than a knowledge of literary associations.

From *Encyclopaedia of Oil Painting Materials and Techniques* by
Frederick Palmer, Batsford, 1984.

An extract from *Aesthetic* by Georges Seurat.

Art is Harmony. Harmony is the analogy of contrary and of similar elements of *tone*, of *colour* and of *line*, considered according to their dominants and under the influence of light, in gay, calm or sad combinations.

The contraries are:

For *tone*, a more $\left\{\begin{array}{l}\text{luminous}\\\text{lighter}\end{array}\right.$ shade against a darker.

For *colour*, the complementaries i.e. a certain red opposed to its complementary, etc. (red-green; orange-blue; yellow-violet).

For *line*, those forming a right angle.

Gaiety of *tone*, is given by the luminous dominant: of *colour*, by the warm dominant; of *line*, by lines above the horizontal.

Calm of *tone*, is given by an equivalence of light and dark; of *colour*, by an equivalence of warm and cold; and of *line*, by horizontals.

Sadness of *tone*, is given by the dominance of dark; of *colour*, by the dominance of cold colours; and of *line*, by downward directions.

From Seurat to *Beaubourg*, 28 August 1890, *La Renaissance du
sentiment, classique*, Paris 1931.

Primary source material

At this stage students could be asked to collect material for their own painting. They might assemble a still-life with objects which evoke their chosen aspect of the theme by their colour and associations, or they may wish to make drawings and colour notations of people and places if it is their intention to create a figure composition. Drawings in museums and galleries might also be undertaken.

Working, methods, materials and media would be decided.

Secondary source material

In preparation for the next stage students could assemble their own supportive material in terms of photographs, newspaper and magazine cuttings, advertisements and videos. This could be part of a homework programme, as could historical and contextual research, and the reading of appropriate poems, prose and plays.

Synthesis

This is the stage when students begin their final piece of work using their analytical material i.e. observational drawings, working sketch-

Far left and left Ancestors of Christ: Aminadab and Naasson his son. *1190. Stained glass windows. 1.40 × 0.51 m (each). Great West Window, Christ Church Cathedral, Canterbury*

Above Gertrude Bell, Daughter of the Desert. *Joanna Buxton. Tapestry. Courtesy of the artist. (See page 26.)*

es, colour and composition notes. Working from these and also from actual objects they begin to create their final statement, their resolution to the problem, the synthesis of their research, preparation and ideas.

Development

Consideration of possible developments might be undertaken by some students willing and able to explore cross-cultural and cross-curricular links. For some it may well be appropriate to pursue aspects and details of their work in terms of extensions into textiles, printmaking or three-dimensional construction. Although less common in schools at the present time, the possibilities of development into film and video could be exciting extensions, as could research into how the theme has been treated in cultures and countries other than our own. Such investigation may well lead into other, more personally selected, projects.

Evaluation

General discussion concerning to what degree the aims and objectives of the project have been achieved could be undertaken in conjunction with the individual's self-assessment. Issues to be considered for evaluation and self-assessment would include comment on the following:

1 Motivation. The understanding of, and reponse to, the project requirements, aims and objectives.
2 Use of resources.
3 Response to primary sources. Observation and visual analysis.
4 Response to secondary sources. Research and use of reference materials.
5 Use and understanding of formal elements.
6 Use and understanding of materials.
7 Selection of appropriate working procedures, media and techniques.
8 Extension of ideas through considered working processes into a final statement.
9 Personal interpretation (including technical skills).
10 Critical analysis and contextual appreciation.
11 Organisation.
12 Confidence.

This general investigation, beginning with an expressive response and moving through the consideration of some aspects of colour and composition to the production of a personal statement is, of course, only one way of working within this theme. More specific aspects could be taken. For example, the expression of joy and sorrow in:

■ the work of one artist;
■ the work of one country, culture, or period;
■ popular culture;
■ the mass media;
■ the visual and performing arts;
■ two-dimensional and three-dimensional objects;
■ male and female artists;
■ symbolic art.

The comparative approach given in the section on portraits has a number of suggested projects which would be applicable not only to this theme, but to many of the others in this book. To avoid repetition they are printed only in the portraits section.

Above *Chinese Dragon Dance. New Year Greeting Card. 1987*

Projects

Portraits

The theme of portraits is, along with still-life and landscape, one of the most explored and popular in the school art department. People, be they strangers, colleagues or ourselves, fascinate us as the wealth of portraits from all ages and most cultures shows. Young people are particularly conscious of their appearance and those aspects of self-adornment which reflect current fashion and help them relate to their peer group and to those public figures whom they admire and emulate. This interest is one which may be the starting point for work which will extend, both in practical and theoretical terms, beyond the drawing of a member of the group into the broader, historical and cultural context, and consequently across the curriculum, developing the student's ability to observe and acquire technical facility into a curiosity about ideas, an interest in research and serious attempts at critical appraisal.

Before we accept the common practice of sitting a member of the class on a chair as a model, perhaps we should ask ourselves and our students questions concerning portraits, and in discussion engender an enthusiasm and enquiry about less usual aspects of the subject.

Obviously the model can be made more unusual and therefore more interesting by being altered in some way: made-up, given a striking accessory, a hat, helmet or piece of equipment, placed in an unexpected setting or dressed differently. The broader questions of how and why costume has altered over the centuries, is different in cultures other than our own may also be raised and could develop into a discussion on how what we wear affects how we feel, move and behave. The extension into issues of dress and gender and the role of men and women is a logical one.

It is often possible to bring people into the school to become, not just passive models, but active participants in a project. As well as the obvious figures in uniform – the policeman, fireman, postman, traffic warden – why not people from the local adult institute, community centre or people's home to talk about their lives and maybe the changes in the local environment whilst they are being drawn, painted or modelled? In this way it would be possible to extend the project on portraits into an investigation of such areas as:

- People and age.
- The different expectations and experiences of men and women.
- How the locality and its inhabitants have altered within a lifetime.
- How society deals with and presents images of, people of different types, cultural backgrounds and ages.

Above Studio portrait. Photograph c. 1900. Private collection

Top Four photographs showing a woman at different ages. Private collection

Above Busking Miner. *Helen Muspratt. 1929. Courtesy of the photographer*

Areas of study

- What is a portrait?
- How does a portrait differ from other representations of head or figure?
- How do we see ourselves?
- How do we wish to see ourselves?
- How do we view our friends and colleagues?
- How do we look at those we admire and also at those in whom we are less interested?
- To what extent does prejudice affect our reaction?
- To what degree does the appearance of those seen affect our response?
- In what ways do people alter? Intentionally? Unintentionally?
- How do we view people of different ages?
- How are people of different ages depicted in painting, sculpture, advertising, illustration, television, film and theatre and in non-visual media such as novels, poems and newspaper reports?
- How are different age groups treated by society?
- When we create portraits of different people what do we want to show?
- How are different ages and social types portrayed in the art of other cultures?
- What are the technical problems we will encounter in the project?
- What are the organisational problems?
- How do we place the figure?
- How do we choose the figure?
- How do we light the figure?
- Why do we select head, head and shoulders or full figure?
- What are the reasons for selecting the viewpoint?
- Why do we place the figure indoors or outside?
- Why do we draw, paint, photograph and model portraits in school?

Many portraits have a purpose. For example:

- Family record. To celebrate lineage or keep memories.
- To impress a suitor or possible spouse.

27

- As a keepsake or remembrance.
- To commemorate an occasion: birth, ceremony, visit, victory, marriage, death.
- To inform authority, provide identification: a passport.
- To impose authority. To impress with the power of church, state, commerce or family.

Areas of study

The subject is so common and so vast a range of examples exist that the combinations and permutations appear endless. Each class situation is different and so a breakdown into acceptable and appropriate approaches will depend on teacher and students. The following areas of study are only suggestions, not definitive lines of enquiry and obviously should be considered in relationship to the practical work undertaken.

A broad based historical survey would be inappropriate and unwieldy and so chronological and cultural aspects of the theme might be better dealt with and related to the student's work by a more comparative approach.

1 Eurocentric

Comparisons between portraits from different European countries, schools of painting and sculpture, and historical periods which would include architectural details and decoration, fashion and design, popular culture and folk art.

2 Cross-cultural

East and West
Europe East and West
Europe and America
Christian – Muslim – Hindu – Buddhist

Below Monument to Balzac. *Auguste Rodin. 1898. Bronze. 300 × 120 × 120 cm. Rodin Museum, Paris*

Bottom right Old Mr Cartwright. *British School. Oil on panel. 78.5 × 62.5 cm. Dulwich Picture Gallery, London*

Left Christ Mocked. *Hieronymus Bosch. Active 1480–1516. Oil on wood panel. 73.7 × 59.1 cm. National Gallery, London*

Above Buddha. *Indonesia. Bronze. Height 10 cm. Private collection*

3 Two-dimensional and three-dimensional

Drawings and engravings
Paintings and prints
Embroidery
Paper currency
Postage stamps
Film, video, photography

Sculpture
Architectural details
Masks and puppets
Coins
Medallions
Ritual and theatrical make-up
and hairstyles

Top Siva. Indonesia. Bronze. Height 25 cm. Private collection

Above Ship's figurehead. National Maritime Museum, Greenwich

Right Stamps

4 Fine art and popular art

Paintings (drawings and prints)

Photography, film and video

Popular prints
Cartoons and comics (including
photo stories)
Advertisements
Fairground and amusment arcade
images
Pub signs
Package labels

Sculpture and constructions	Dolls
	Masks
Three-dimensional assemblages	Puppets
	Porcelain figurines
	Souvenir models
	Toby jugs

5 Information or decoration?

Certain images may be easily placed in these two categories, for example, official paintings, sculpture and photographs, political leaflets and posters, television images and family snapshots may all give information and have been created to do so, but they may with time have ceased to be valuable as conveyors of information and become decorative. Examples of portraits as decoration are not difficult to find, particularly if we look to popular art, advertising and the media e.g. pub signs, magazine covers, container labels. There are, though, those portraits which may fall into both categories, or about which it is difficult to decide, for example:

Egyptian coffin portraits
Equestrian statues
Portraits on coins, notes and stamps
Persian miniatures
Mughal paintings
Japanese prints
Medieval manuscripts
Elizabethan portraits which include symbols relating to the sitter

Above Matilda, Queen of England, AD 1100–18. Romanesque seal. 80 × 55 cm. Dean and Chapter of Durham Cathedral

Below Indian rickshaw painting. Twentieth century

6 Commerce and propaganda

It could be argued that these two areas are too similar for consideration, indeed at times interchangeable, but a stimulating number of comparisons might be found by looking at such things as:

Religious paintings of various cultures
Political pamphlets and cartoons

Above Guy Fawkes and friends at Charing Cross Underground station, London

Above left The Durbar of Thakur Nawal Singh of Pali. *Rajasythan, Marwar (Jodhpur) School c. 1825. Opaque watercolour on paper. 35.1 × 45 cm. Collection Terence McInerney, New York*

Above *Pub signs*

Below *Political pamphlets*

Middle right *Wrapped theatre*

Bottom right An Unknown Couple in a Landscape. *Gainsborough. Oil on canvas. 76.2 × 67.0 cm. Dulwich Picture Gallery, London*

War posters as well as product and event posters
Record sleeves and concert announcements
Satirical drawings and theatrical acts
Packaging

7 Portraits in interior and exterior settings

Questions about the relationship between sitter and setting could reveal ideas about image presentation, emotional expression, property ownership, character presentation and also spectator reaction. A look at film, television and advertising in this way would also be informative.

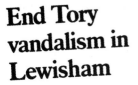

8 Single and multiple images

An investigation into why the portrait presenter chooses to use single or multiple images of a person could help students to consider their own ideas about portraits, the importance of viewpoint, the various ways in which the third dimension can be depicted and the importance of means other than a straight forward portrait showing sitters and their attributes. Single images abound. A look at the following will be a useful starting point for research into the use of multiple images.

- Sketchbooks, notebooks and worksheets.
- Paintings depicting the life of a particular person e.g. *Four Scenes from the Early Life of S. Zenobius* by Sandro Botticelli, National Gallery, London. *Sir Henry Unton, (c1596)* by an unknown artist, National Portrait Gallery, London.

Right Egyptian coffin, British Museum, London

Below Molly Longlegs. George Stubbs. Walker Art Gallery, Liverpool

Left Triple Portrait of Richleiu. Champaigne. 1642. A painting showing three aspects of the head on a canvas to be sent to the sculptor Fransesco Mocchi in Rome, who was commissioned to make a portrait bust of the cardinal, National Gallery, London

Bottom Life of Sir Henry Unton. Unknown artist. c. 1596. Panel. 74.0 × 163.2 cm. National Portrait Gallery, London

To what extent these and similar paintings are portraits is an interesting debatable point. Other less contentious examples are: *Triple Portrait of Richelieu* by Champaigne, National Gallery, London; many paintings and pastels by Edgar Degas; the photographs of Marey, Duchamp and Muybridge which show figures in movement; the Cubist and Futurist portraits which contain simultaneous viewpoints of the sitter and; of course, frames from films, stills from video and blurred and superimposed photographs. The photographic collages of David Hockney are also valuable in this context.

Two further, more controversial categories come to mind:

- Formal – Expressive
- Figurative – Abstract

Both rely heavily on personal opinion and interpretation and are fraught with difficulties of definition. For example, a portrait may have both formal and expressive attributes, contain qualities which some will consider classical and others romantic. Similarly, to what extent may a portrait be 'abstracted' before it becomes non-figurative? Into which area could be placed a painting such as Malevich's *Portrait of an Englishman in Moscow* and to what degree is an Impressionist portrait an abstraction from nature?

These contentious categories, with their arguable titles and examples are given here as 'extras', areas of study whose idiosyncratic character should stimulate the student to suggestions no less personal and debatable.

9 Formal and expressive (Classical and Romantic?)

Greek and Roman busts	Gothic sculpture
Velasquez	Goya
Ingres	Delacroix
Reynolds	Rowlandson
Degas	Renoir
Cézanne	Soutine

Whereas the above may be placed in the two categories even though they may raise questions, where do we place the following?

Assyrian and Egyptian sculpture	Gainsborough
African masks	El Greco
Eastern temple carving	Hockney and Kitaj
Titian	Society and business portraits
Rembrandt	and those in magazines and on television?

10 Figurative and abstract (abstracted from rather than non-figurative)

Greco-Roman sculpture	Egyptian, African and Assyrian statues
Renaissance popes and nobles	
Flemish primitives	Francis Bacon
Rembrandt, Hals, Vermeer	Modigliani
Impressionist portraits	Soutine, Picasso, Matisse
David Hockney	de Kooning and American Expressionists
Andy Warhol	
Contemporary photographs	German Expressionists
Official statues	Cubism
Posters	Giacometti
	Grafitti

There is no need for these to be paired or polarised as they appear here and the questions they promote may well be dealt with more easily by taking different ideas of 'likeness' as a point of departure.

a Representational likeness is often sought when a historical record is required. In such instances verisimilitude is of major importance, but some features may be idealised for the sake of vanity, or they may be exaggerated for humour. For example: Renaissance works, Elizabethan miniatures, Reynolds, Ingres, David, society portrait painters, Hockney and Green.

b For some artists the *expression* of more intangible qualities may be as, or more, important and so selection and manipulation of the seen, combined with appropriate working methods, will allow the desired emotion, mood or aura to be achieved. The artist's personal choice may mean the omission of inessentials and the exaggeration of selected aspects which enhance those qualities the artist is intent on communicating, for example, the sadness, contentment, movement or power of the sitter. In such works the setting and accessories may be used to symbolise, offset or express aspects of the character. For example: Goya, Schiele, Dix, Picasso, Sutherland, Bacon.

c In some instances the abstract qualities which the artist sees in a particular sitter may become of prime importance and the more obvious appearance or superficial likeness disappear. The portrait becomes an arrangement of lines, shapes, colours and forms which have been inspired by the sitter and which may or may not convey some aspect of character or poise. For example: Picasso (Cubist period), Gris, Malevich, Delaunay, Moore, Gaudier-Brezeska.

Self-portrait

A project on portraits will probably look at self-portraits which raises additional questions. For example:

- What do we see when we look at ourselves in a mirror? Is it what we wish to see?
- What do our friends see? What do we see in their mirrors?
- Does the mirror image differ in any way from the real image?
- How have we changed over the years?
- How have we appeared at various stages of our lives: baby, toddler, child, teenager?
- How can we change our appearance now? e.g. clothes, hats, wigs, jewellery, spectacles, make-up. Why do we wear these things?
- In what ways do the clothes we wear in school differ from those we wear for leisure? Why is this?
- How is our appearance affected by current fashion and by what our friends think and wear?

Our clothes, the contents of pockets, and bags say something about us. The things we carry around with us, as well as what we collect and the interests we have, can be incorporated into a portrait to give more information about identity. The link with coats of arms, flags, banners and heraldry in general, could be developed in this way. These may not only be limited to individuals but extend into family and clan regions, country symbols and the trade marks, logos, crests and badges used as signs of recognition by industrial and commercial

Above Self-portrait. *Dame Ethel Walker. c. 1925. National Portrait Gallery, London*

34

Above left *Sheet of photographs from a photo booth*

Above right Bede, Commentary on the Apocolypse. St John with Scribe. *Ramsey Abbey, 1160–70. Ink on vellum. 27.0 × 17.8 cm. St John's College, Cambridge. The scribe kneels at the feet of St John, author of the Apocolypse, dressed as a bishop. The lower inscription reads 'The scribe of this book (begs) pardon.'*

firms, as well as those emblems associated with public office, the military and religious orders, their costumes and accoutrements.

Some painters have left a record of themselves, how they looked at different times and how age altered them, for example, Rembrandt, Van Gogh (and letters), Cézanne, Bacon, Titian, Courbet, Gauguin, Degas and Hockney. A display of such pictures alongside photographs from family albums would make a good starting point for discussion.

Drawings and paintings could be done in conjunction with photographic booth self-portraits. Autobiography is also a form of self-portrait, as is a diary which records thoughts and ideas as well as events and appointments. Written self-portraits would give an added dimension to the project and research into similar endeavours by artists and writers could be a valuable educational experience making links with other subject areas such as English, history, sociology and the humanities in general.

The Environment

The environment is used constantly as a resource in art and design education and is considered not just convenient, but educationally valuable. The popularity of the Art and the Built Environment Project is evidence of this, as is the response to the School Curriculum Development Committee's Teachers' Fund. Ten per cent of the applications received were for schemes dealing with some aspect of environmental education.

Left *Places to live*

Below *Albert Square, Manchester. Pierre Valette. City Art Gallery, Manchester*

Teachers are keenly aware of the potential of environmental studies, a potential that has been summarised as education:

FROM the environment – a resource of information and opportunities for direct experience.

ABOUT the environment – to develop pupils' knowledge and understanding of the nature of the environment.

FOR the environment – to encourage feelings, attitudes and awareness of the environment.

These aspects, and there may be more, are closely interrelated, indeed often inseparable in any teaching programme and they may apply to the natural or man-made environment.

From: SCDC publication LINK, Autumn term 1985.

Any project taking the environment as a theme must be structured to local needs and to the students' interests and requirements, which means thoughtful selection of ideas and course planning on the part of the teacher. The topic is too wide to be offered without such organisation ranging, as it does, in terms of subject from city to architectural details, with social, political, historical and economic considerations and allowing for ways of working from interpretation to problem-solving design.

If a major project, with cross-curricular links, and perhaps more than one interrelated modular course, is envisaged, then it might be advisable to make use of those agencies which, both nationally and locally, are prepared to contribute to work in schools. In addition to subject advisors, regional arts associations, local town planning bodies and councils, there are such schemes as the Architects in Schools organised by the Royal Institute of British Architects and Craftspeople in Schools run by the Crafts Council. Local industries, museums, galleries and the Department of the Environment are also worth contacting for additional support.

Areas of study
The city

Under this heading are eight possible projects which are obviously related and may be used with one another.

1 Art and the city

- Influences of the city on art and of art on the city.
- Representation of the city in various art forms, media and countries.

2 The city and society

- Visual comment (painting, sculpture, film, television, photography) on the city as a reflection of society.
- The effect of the city on people i.e. the social benefits and problems; amenities and deficiencies. Related social comment through dance, drama, opera etc.

Below Canal Scene. *Spencer Gore. York City Art Gallery*

Bottom Liverpool Landscape. *George Kennerley. Merseyside County Art Galleries*

3 Urban structures

- The city as: community centre, fortification, commercial centre, leisure centre, theatre.
- Consideration of zones and traffic flow, precincts and wasteland.

4 'Painting and sculpture' in the city

- Official sculpture and decoration, monuments and statues, murals and relief sculpture.
- Posters for advertising and information.
- Road signs, popular art, neon signs, graffiti.

Left Mural on a building in Greenwich

Below Public sculpture

Top right Notre Dame L'Ille de la Cité, *The British Library, London*

Bottom right A scene from the science fiction city in the film 'Blade Runner'

5 The city and twentieth–century art

Relationships between the two, for example, the influence of, and on the city of, Cubism, Futurism, de Stijl, the Bauhaus and Pop Art, sculpture, film, television and video.

6 Design and the city

- Historical and geographical research into different types of cities, their design and growth.
- Design layout related to urban functions e.g. fortification, trading port, traffic flow.
- Industrial design: street furniture, transport, bridges etc.
- Graphic design: verbal and non-verbal communication, sign and symbol, information relay.
- Ideal cities of the past. Utopias.

7 Mass media and the city

- The effect of the city on the media, and of the media on the city.
- The media as a reflection of and/or an escape from the city.

8 The city of the future

- 'Fantastic' architecture. New materials and forms of construction.
- The possible requirements of urban society in the twenty-first century.
- Science fiction cities.
- Cities in space.

District

Some of the ideas which are listed under the city heading might be incorporated into a study of a more specific area. The theme of district could be used for work based on a neighbourhood, a street, the school or the home. In addition to the practical work such a project would involve the use of local libraries, archives and record offices as well as departments of the local council. Assistance from architects, builders, the police, transport authorities and commercial companies might also be incorporated. Photography, video and tape recordings would be important elements in such a project.

1 Research into drawings, photographs and maps showing the changes which have occurred over the years could, in conjunction with the student's visual studies, raise questions of how and for what reasons alterations have been made. A logical extension would be to investigate current and forthcoming developments, to ascertain problems and attempt to provide solutions.

2 Classification of buildings in terms of period, style and function might also be undertaken, not simply as a means of compiling a catalogue, but as a basis for consideration of what aesthetic, social, industrial or economic reasons helped to determine the location of buildings and the materials used in their construction. The relationship between appearance and function could also be an aspect worth exploring.

3 A study of the facilities provided in the district for the people living, working and playing there would reveal the disposition of road layouts, underpasses, bridges, markets and shopping areas, parks, recreational facilities and the social, religious and educational amenities. Each of these could be considered separately in connection with the requirements of people of different ages, occupations, interests and social groups.

4 The issue of renovation versus demolition, especially if related to a district with buildings of historic and/or visual importance, would be worth pursuing with collaboration from local councils and private architects, surveyors, building contractors, solicitors and house agents, and any arts or preservation organisations concerned. Research into past schemes of local historical, archaeological or geographical conservation and general renovation and replacement would add further dimensions. Agencies worth contacting include the Department of the Environment, the National Trust, English Heritage, the Heritage Education Trust, and the Building Preservation Trust based at Hampton Court Palace.

Above The Courtyard of a House in Delft. *Pieter de Hoogh. 1658. Oil on canvas. 73.5 × 60.0 cm. National Gallery, London*

Far right top *Cornfield with combined harvester, Norfolk*

Far right centre *Mohamed Moussa, Wissa Wassef Art School. 1984. Tapestry. 3.60 × 2.50 m. Photo by Werner Forman*

Right Rama, Lakshmana and Sita in Panchavati. *Illustration to the Ramayana Mughal, sub-imperial style. c. 1595. Opaque watercolour on paper heightened with gold. 28.6 × 19.1 cm. Private collection, London*

Country, seaside and gardens

Country

In addition to the normal landscape studies based on the local environment, field and holiday trips, perhaps undertaken with the history and geography departments, allow more detailed investigation. Studies might include one or more of the following:

1 Types of landscape e.g. mountains, escarpments, rivers, lakes, estuaries, fens, forestry, woodland, downland, moorland, arable and grazing land.

2 The inhabitants' relationship with the landscape.

3 The respresentation of landscape and its influence locally and possibly nationally, on art and design. For example, eighteenth and nineteenth-century topographical drawing and painting: the Norwich School and the St Ives group.

4 An examination of a particular landscape feature and its treatment in painting, sculpture and design. For example, mountains – British, Indian, Chinese and contemporary land artists.

Right Harvest Moon. *Samuel Palmer. British Museum, London*

5 A study of the various ways people have imposed themselves on the landscape. For example:
- farm complexes;
- isolated and grouped cottages;
- villages and hamlets;
- market towns;
- country houses and parkland (stately homes and royal palaces);
- market gardens;
- monasteries, abbeys, priories, churches;
- temples and burial grounds;
- land art e.g. Christo's wrapped and curtained landscapes, Greg Bright's mazes, Richard Long's involvement in and of landscape, Andy Goldsworthy's landscape constructions.

Seaside

Initial discussion might consider various aspects of the theme such as seaports, fishing ports, commercial centres, holiday towns, playgrounds, and retirement homes, and select from these broad definitions group or individual areas of study.

Alternatively, specific details of the seaside environment might be taken as the theme for a project. For example:

- seaside architecture;
- docklands;
- piers;

Below Blackpool looking south from the Tower

- amusment arcades, fairgrounds, beach activities, sports facilities;
- theatres and cinemas;
- parks and gardens;
- promenades and esplanades;
- shipyards;
- fish markets;
- new estates, bungalows and caravan parks, hotels and holiday homes;
- seaside souvenirs;
- holiday costumes.

Gardens

Aspects of natural and man-made design are all contained within the theme, as are the possibilities of cross-cultural relationships and cross-curricular links with history, geography, science, mathematics, botany, biology, literature and music. In addition, developments could be encouraged which considered colour manufacture, paper making, basketry, weaving with natural materials, food, cosmetics, perfumery, medicine, dyes, herbs and floristry, landscape gardening, and furniture and implement design.

Top *The Rain, it Raineth Everyday. Norman Garstin. 1889. Penzance Town Council*

Above *Radha and Krishna seek Shelter from the Rain. Rsjasthan, Bundi School. c. 1680. Opaque watercolour on paper. 28.0 × 17.0 cm. Private collection, Geneva*

- Historical and geographical survey e.g. Far Eastern, Chinese, Japanese, Moorish, Persian, Caribbean and European gardens: their design and purpose, their use as inspiration and their influence abroad in terms of all aspects of art and design.
- City gardens: public and private, park and roof.
- Suburban gardens.

- English cottage gardens: social developments affecting looks and use.
- British country houses: garden and park, house and setting.
- Royal gardens.
- Garden centres.
- Flower gardens. Fruit and flower stalls, horticultural shows.
- Vegetable gardens.
- Arboreta (links with forestry and river authorities).
- Botanical gardens.
- Tropical gardens.
- Zoological gardens.
- Conservatories and greenhouses.
- Courtyards and terraces.
- Plant containers: window boxes, indoor containers, pots for terrace and yard.
- Formal gardens.
- Romantic gardens.
- Winter gardens.
- Topiary.
- Orchards.
- Gardens expressing different cultures e.g. Persian, Caribbean, paradise gardens, Garden of Eden, magic gardens, dream gardens Tree of Life.
- Water gardens, lakes, ponds, fountains, waterfalls.
- Garden architecture e.g. follies, summer houses, gazebos.
- Plant and flower symbolism.

Practical and research work based on comparative appraisal, influences, interpretations and the solving of design problems with all that is thereby implied, in terms of form and colour, texture and pattern organisation, are all possible and perhaps self-evident within this theme.

Environmental design project

In addition, or as an alternative to using the environment as a resource for interpretive work, a particular design project could be agreed which allowed the students to investigate an area or site, ascertain the deficencies or requirements and propose solutions to inherent design problems. The following factors might be useful when planning such a project.

Investigation of the site

- What are the assets and deficiencies of the location?
- What are the problems to occupants, operatives and the general public?
- Have solutions to the problems been previously implemented? Are they successful? If so, then how? If not, why not?
- Do the problems relate to construction, communication, machines and transport, as well as to individuals and society in general?

Recording on site

The gathering of information about the current state of the site by whatever means is appropriate and available e.g. drawing, painting, photography, filming, and the use of video and sound tape recording.

Assessment of information

Cataloguing, filing or organising the information collected by whatever means possible.

Requirements

- What will further research and development requirements be?
- What materials and technical support will be needed?
- What will be required in order to evaluate successfully? e.g. questionnaires, public opinion, specialist evaluation, course assessment?

Development of collected information

Initial drawings and sketches of ideas leading to more finished designs.

Design prototype

Completed designs transferred into technical drawings. Three-dimensional prototypes in suitable materials to allow for spatial evaluation.

Construction

The construction of the final model with back-up material showing process and design development and written assessment of problems and solutions.

Evaluation

Individual assessment, tutorial and group discussion. How does the final solution fulfil the initial aim?

Some environmental design areas

- Suburban railway station
- Bus waiting area
- Airport lounge, reception and departure areas
- Modular living areas
- Modular houseboats, caravan units and parks
- School for children with special needs e.g. handicapped
- Animal feeding area
- Shopping precinct
- Food, cattle, retailing market area
- Sports arena
- General classroom
- Recreational area for school
- Leisure complex for local use

- City river frontage
- Village centre
- Town square
- Pedestrian walkways
- Car parking facilities
- Park and playground
- Estate for the elderly
- Industrial zone
- Commercial complex
- Harbour and port amenities
- Farming complex
- Transport intersections
- Hotel complex
- Cemetery and cremetorium area
- Hospital complex

A structured programme, organising study skills (experiential, perceptual, research, conceptual, critical, communication and evaluative) could be created to concentrate on particular details of the environment; some concerned with architecture, some with construction and some with the infra-structure. For example details of:

Doorways	Staircases
General entrances	Precincts
Windows	Subways
Chimneys	Monuments
Walls	Fences and railings
Roofs	Corners
Floors	Signs

Constructional methods and materials related to the above and to the following:

Roads	Railways
Bridges	Canals

Above *Harem, Topkapi Palace, Istanbul. Second half of sixteeenth century. Photograph by*
Dr Ahmet Ertug/Zamana Gallery, London. (see page 50)

Interiors

As with any project theme interiors could be approached in a broad historical, geographical, economic or social manner, but such a survey is probably as unwieldy as it is obvious. However, these implications will be an integral part of any study which considers specific aspects of the theme. There is considerable resource material available; we spend a great deal of our lives in interiors, we visit other houses and go into shops, cafes, restaurants, clubs, cinemas, theatres and schools. Museums and galleries contain representations and reconstructions of interiors from other times and places and are themselves interiors which are worth more thought than we normally give them. The interior architecture, design, decoration and layout of shops and department stores are also often overlooked and would be a valuable resource for work on interiors. Bookstalls abound with magazines dealing with the theme in terms of design and decoration. There is no shortage of resources – selection is the problem.

Below Henry Moore's studio

Bottom Portrait of Duranty. *Edgar Degas. Burrell Collection, Glasgow*

The room as a reflection of a person

Most people like to surround themselves with objects and decor with which they are at ease and which, in some measure, show their personality. A 'room of one's own' is a common human aspiration although it may not always be possible to achieve. Indications of personality may occur in a room over a period of time, almost haphazardly, without planned thought of the final effect but rather as an accumulation of items reflecting interests or the momentary succumbing to whim or fashion. The 'teenager's' room often grows in this way with a wealth of pop images, posters, record sleeves, magazines, books, audio and video systems, clothes and personal accessories. It is a ready-made resource for a project looking at an interior as a reflection of its occupant, with possible extensions into interior design and decoration with aspects of colour, pattern and texture; or visual and written analysis of the personal collection of objects and images.

Creative artists in all media are aware of the importance of interior settings as a means of commenting upon the people portrayed. We find examples of painters carefully recording rooms in which their sitters have their portraits painted, for example, Holbein's *The*

Ambassadors, National Gallery, London with its green damask curtaining, 'Turkey' carpet, paved floor (the design of which is a variation of one in Westminster Abbey) and two-tiered table on which has been assembled a still-life reflecting the pursuits of the two men portrayed: globes, books, hymnals, scientific and musical instruments. Similarly, Manet painted the writer Emile Zola with his books, quill pen, reproductions of a Japanese print (a contemporary fashion) and his own painting *Olympia*. Degas's portrait of his friend Duranty, surrounded by books and pamphlets on table and shelves, is a precursor of the television setting which so often accompanies an interview with a writer or academic.

Advertisements also place people in conjunction with interiors and objects which it is believed will reflect the type of person presented and naturally their involvement with the product being sold.

The room as an expression of a person

Few of us have the opportunity, the time and money to create a room which we believe fully expresses our character, perhaps few of us have the inclination to do so, but some people seem to manage to make a completely overt statement about themselves in a conscious way. We can find examples of this in magazines and newspapers. Photographs and articles on the houses and apartments of wealthy or well-known people, and also on the interiors created for them by professional designers, are constantly being presented to us in the media and are evidence of our curiosity about how other people live. Although we may not have the means or desire to create rooms as expressions of ourselves, we can alter and invent in drawing, painting and construction, photographic montage and printing.

The room as an indication of mood

In many respects this is an integral part of the previous two sections, for the unconsidered collection of objects and the decoration, governed by whatever restrictions or chance, will create a mood, as may the individual's conscious attempt to communicate an expression of individuality through considered design. The uses of a room will also determine a mood. Places of entertainment, a library, gym, interiors for work or worship will all have their peculiarities which create a mood. Advertisers are well aware of the importance of mood as are designers for theatre, film and television, creating as they do sets to reinforce character and emphasise action. Painters as diverse as Vermeer and Munch, de Hooch and Vuillard, Bonnard and Bacon have likewise communicated the mood of their interior settings, either when they have treated them as subjects in themselves, or as indications of the emotions of the people represented.

Above The Laden Table. *Edouard Vuillard. c. 1908. Pastel. 47.0 × 54.5 cm. Tate Gallery, London.* © *DACS 1988*

Areas of study

- Interiors related to specific purposes, for example:
  Relaxation – sitting room, theatre, cinema.
  Work – school, factory, garage, hospital, studio, kitchen, shop, office.
  Worship – cathedral, church, mosque, synagogue, temple.
  Culture – art galleries, museums, historic houses, concert halls.
  Leisure – sports arenas, swimming pools, zoos, aquaria.

Some of these examples fall into more than one category e.g. places of worship may also be places of culture and, of course, what is a relaxing interior for one person may be a place of work for another.

- Private and public interiors – caravan, town hall, studio, factory, bedroom, supermarket, dining-room, restaurant.
- Interiors, and their depiction in art and the media, as social

Above The Dissolute Household, *Jan Steen. Oil on canvas. Victoria and Albert Museum, London*

comment, for example, Vermeer, Vuillard, Sickert, Doré, film documentaries, television programmes, newspaper photographs.
■ Theatre, film and television sets related to story and action.

It is not just the news and documentary items on television which make social comment or reflect social problems and attitudes. Consideration should also be given to those series and serials, soap operas and situation comedies, which emphasise, as well as indicate, the background and lifestyle of the characters in the story. Further critical consideration leading to practical work could deal with how the interior (and exterior) settings are representative of the people portrayed; how much is reality and how much fantasy; what appears to be real, and what reinforces our notion of the real.

The idea of reality and illusion related to the theme of interiors might be continued in terms of theatre in its many forms. A look at the interiors of theatres, cinemas, concert halls, circuses and similar establishments will lead quite naturally into an interest in the theatrical setting. This may be developed into set design, the making of toy and puppet theatres and the construction of dolls houses, or models of interiors relating to design problems. For example:

- The design of a particular interior by the invention of a space suited to its function or the alteration of an existing space.
- The decoration of the interior with both functional and decorative items.

A programme for such a scheme of work might be itemised and, at each stage, incorporate educational objectives, basic elements of art and design, working procedures and relevant practices.

- Selection of space, actual or invented, related to its purpose.
- Identification of problems.
- Research into similar interior spaces (historically, geographically, contemporary) noting how problems have been resolved in different ways and the space made relevant to the occupiers.
- Decision about materials to be used in the next stage.
- Drawings of the interior space showing parts to be retained, extended or removed with details of windows, doorways, stairs etc.
- Decisions about materials to be used in the next stage.
- Prototype model.
- Evaluation of problem resolution to date.
- Selection or design of:
  colour scheme;
  patterns and textures;
  fabrics;
  floor covering;
  furniture;
  lighting (type and fittings);
  heating (type and fittings);
  detailed fixtures and fittings e.g. washing, cooking facilities, switches, sockets etc.
- Evaluation in relation to initial objectives.

Above Train Landscape. *Eric Ravillious. Aber* *Art Gallery and Museums.* © *Estate of Eric Rav* *1988, all rights reserved DACS*

Below left Period room. Geffrye Museum, London

Below right Derelict church

The scope for cross-curricular cooperation is obvious, as is the opportunity for involving outside agencies and expertise. Such expertise could include professional interior designers, lecturers from college departments of industrial design and art and design history, as well as experts from museums, architects' offices, local electricity and gas boards, building and decorating firms, and do-it-yourself centres, shops and wholesalers.

An interesting extension to the project could be undertaken with the assistance of the mathematics department and allow the student to cost the original ideas and then work again on the scheme within the restrictions of a limited budget. Costing, loans with interest, hire purchase agreements and similar financial considerations could all be incorporated into the project to the practical benefit of the student.

A shorter and perhaps less ambitious project could be devised around animal houses. On one level this could deal with the needs of different animals in zoos, but on another could grow from a study of the requirements and habits of pet rabbits, mice, hampsters and birds. One virtue of such a scheme is that the student would, in some cases, be able to construct the animal house, rather than having to be content with making models.

Right The Deceitful Heroine. *Basholi Punjab School. c. 1680. Victoria and Albert Museum, London*

Below left Colossal Elephant. *Victorian engraving*

Below right Queen Mary's dolls' house. *1880. Height 97 cm, width 83 cm, depth 39 cm. Given Museum of London. Given to Princess Mary of Teck, later Queen Mary, by her mother Princess Mary Adelaide, Duchess of Teck. Furnished by gifts and purchases over a period of several years. Museum of London*

Above Fan design of 1728–30 showing St Bartholomew's Fair. Etching and aquatint
(coloured) published by J. F. Setchel, 23 King Street, Covent Garden. Museum of London

Kleenex Velvet

Above Sequence from a Kleenex television advertisement. Courtesy of DMB & B

Advertising

Aspects of advertising have been a part of art and design courses for many years and also part of the student's work in other areas of the curriculum. A great deal of what has been done has been isolated within subject categories and yet the nature of the theme is such that a wide range of integrated or linked courses could be devised.

Advertising is not a contemporary phenomenon, although the scope and size of activities and the media developments may be peculiar to this century. A critical awareness of how messages are created and conveyed, how people are influenced and manipulated, are important aspects of education. Any project dealing with advertising will move into those areas of media studies which are currently dealt with in terms of language and content by the English and social studies departments in schools. In most cases the media have strong visual components which should be considered alongside the text or commentary. Media literacy means visual literacy, that is how and

Below Shop window writing

why images are created and used in conjunction with other forms of communication. Historical precedents and connections will form a necessary part of any study.

Areas of study

An investigation of advertising in terms of:

- Similarities and differences.
- Relationship to audience and also to product i.e. form and content.
- Signs and symbols. Trademarks and logos.
- Words and images. Words as images.
- Sounds and images.
- Context e.g. juxtoposition of an advertisement with another or with fiction or factual articles in magazines, newspapers, television; in the home; the street or store.
- Image analysis: how and why has the advertisement been created?
- Portrayal of people e.g. racism, sexism, social status.
- Information and propaganda e.g. political and religious advertisements, state and church, education and indoctrination.

Below Old signs

Above Magazine page. 1901

THE GREAT GLOBE SWANAGE   BY GRAHAM SUTHERLAND

YOU CAN BE SURE OF SHELL

PHOTOGRAPHERS PREFER SHELL

Colour Photograph by Curtis Moffat

YOU CAN BE SURE OF SHELL

Top, centre and bottom left *Shell posters by the graphic designer E. M. Knight Kauffer 1937, the artist Graham Sutherland 1932, and the photographer Curtis Moffat 1934*

Top right *Handbills for performing fleas. c. 1820.*

Bottom right *Poster and figure*

Advertising media and methods

Medium	Methods
Posters and bills	Print, graphics, photography
Press (newspapers and magazines)	Print, graphics, photography
Television	Film, video, sound
Film and video	Film, video, sound
Radio	Sound
Displays	Shop·window, counter, shelf, stand, kiosk, sponsorship
Packaging	Print, graphics, photography

Advertisements appeal to what the advertisers call 'hidden needs', that is those areas of desire which the consumer *feels*, perhaps unknowingly, to be important; obviously at different times, in differing circumstances and related to particular products. The following categories might serve as a basis for an analysis of advertisements. Further divisions could be made in terms of age and sex, as could a comparison of responses from different groups.

Happiness	Friendship
Success	Sexual attraction
Power	Money
Health	Career advancement
Domesicity	Security
Immortality	Romance
Maternity	Paternity
Pride	Sophistication
Femininity	Masculinity
Status	Belonging

There are, of course, other categories and advertisements can attempt to appeal to more than one of the 'hidden needs' listed above.

Above *Coca Cola neon sign*

Right *Man pasting poster*

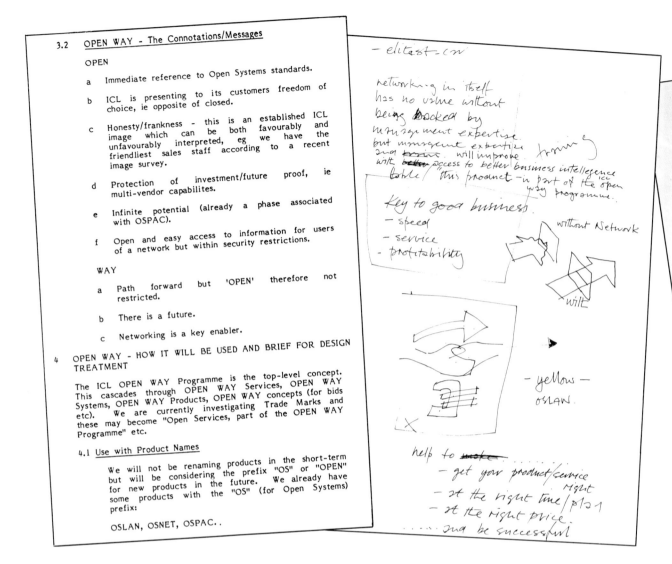

Group project

A mini advertising agency could be set up with small groups of students undertaking some of the roles covered by the different departments of an actual agency. For example:

■ Group discussion and decision on an imaginary product.

This might be done in conjunction with some market research about types of products desired by other students in the school. Separate groups could then work on briefs agreed jointly at a meeting at the start of each session.

Research department

■ Market research.
■ Historical research: what has been done that is similar?
■ Collect and collate information for other groups.
■ Provide relevant charts and graphs etc.

Media department

This could be a number of small groups dealing with the different media. In conjunction with the presentation of the product the actual container and packaging could be designed and created. The writing

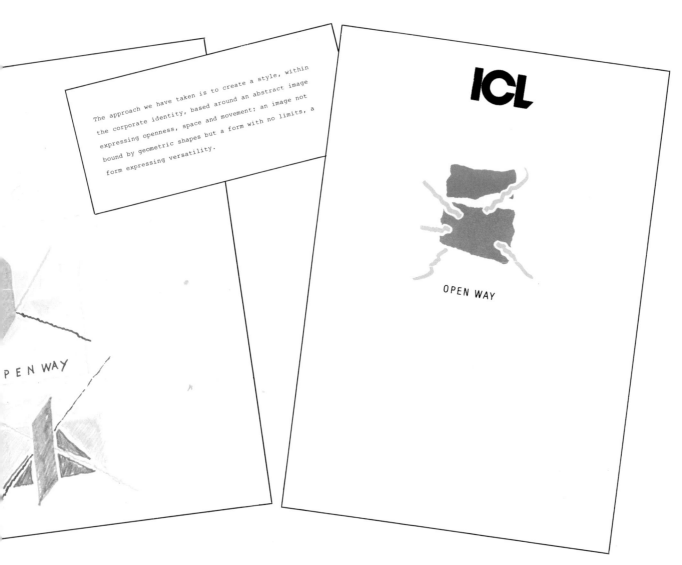

The approach we have taken is to create a style, within the corporate identity, based around an abstract image expressing openness, space and movement; an image not bound by geometric shapes but a form with no limits, a form expressing versatility.

ICL

OPEN WAY

Above both pages Extract from design brief, designers' response, initial sketches and final image. 1987. Client: ICL. Design Group: H & P Associates. Art Director: Nick Coupland. Designers: Shaun Evans and David Magee.

of copy, scripts for film, television and radio would be an important part of this department's work alongside the visual elements of layout, sequence and the relationship between word and image.

Production department

As well as acting as a coordinator for all the participants this department could organise links with outside agencies and arrange visits to relevant places of work. It could also invite into the school specialists to talk to the students working on the project. For example: printers, graphic designers, photographers, film and television programme makers, package designers, illustrators and, of course, people from advertising agencies. Representatives from a client firm would also be interesting and useful contributors to the course.

Accounts department

Although obviously essential in the real world of advertising such a department might be an optional extra in the context of this project, dependent upon the interests and capabilities of the students and the willingness of mathematics colleagues to cooperate.

Such a department might work on the actual financial implications of the project, relating them to the art and design department's capitation or it might work on the basis of estimates received from outside services and organisations.

AN ADVERTISING ELEPHANT.

This ingenious device, which is in use in several Continental cities, and which we may expect to see, in due course, in London, consists of a model of an elephant, provided with a hollow trunk, which is filled with leaflets of advertisements. As the model proceeds along the streets the operator inside the elephant drives the leaflets out in showers from the end of the trunk by means of a piston fitted to the inner end, on the same principle as a boy's pop-gun.

If men had a taste of what most women do, they'd soon be looking into a Cred

Surprising though it may seem, Creda tumble dryers actually help with the ironing.

It's the reverse action that does it; a system whereby the drum changes direction every couple of minutes, thus avoiding the balling-up of clothes, uneven drying and unnecessary creasing.

What's more, in our Debonair Sensair model, there's a sensor that detects the precise level of dryness you require and stops the machine at that point.

A cold tumble follows, leaving garments airing-cupboard fresh and ready to wear (or ready to be given an iron should they need it).

And finally, if you're not there to remove the clothes, the machine will go on tumbling intermittently, so preventing them creasing-up at the bottom of the drum.

All Creda tumble dryers are made in Britain and can be front or rear-vented. Their styling is such that it complements our range of washing machines perfectly.

Mel Smith might be happy to hear that they're also inexpensive to run. A little less than the cost one of those chocolate Wispa ba for every load.

Creda
Science for womankind.

TI CREDA LTD. PR (STM/2) BLYTHE BRIDGE, STOKE ON TRENT STAFFORDSHIRE ST11 9LJ

Top *Advertising elephant. Engraving 1873*

Bottom *Creda advert*

64

讲究卫生，不吸烟，不喝酒，不随地吐痰。

中学生守则 (五)
ZHONG XUE SHENG SHOU ZE

OTHER HANDS WILL TAKE UP THE WEAPONS

ΚΗΔΕΙΑ

Τὴν προσφιλῆν μας Θείαν

ΕΛΕΝΗΝ Δ. ΣΟΥΚΟΥΛΗ

ΕΤΩΝ 100

Θανοῦσαν κηδεύομεν αὔριον Δευτέραν καὶ ὥραν 10 π. μ

Παρακαλοῦμεν πάντας τοὺς συγγενεῖς καὶ φίλους ὅπως εὐαρεστούμενοι συ-νοδεύσωσι τὴν ἐκφορὰν τῆς ἐκ τῆς οἰκίας μας

Ἐν Κορίνθῳ τῇ 31 Ἰουλίου 1960

ΟΙ ΑΝΕΨΙΑ   ΟΙ ΣΥΓΓΕΝΕΙΣ

Αἰκατερίνη Γ. Σούκουλη

Top *Chinese poster*
Bottom left *Cuban political poster*
Bottom right *Greek death announcement*

Celebration

Celebration is a theme which can cover a wide area, only some of which is indicated here. The background and experience of the student will extend the theme in terms of social structures, domestic traditions, religious rituals, political persuasions and community conventions.

In this instance a broad interpretation of the word has been taken to cover some of those areas of study which, although on the fringe of the central theme, are related and of interest to the student. Consequently, aspects of entertainment which might be the subject of a separate project have been included as having an element of celebration within them. It could also be remembered that what is considered a celebration by one group of people, may not be thought so by another. For example, certain religious rites involving forms of sacrifice, some of the Roman games and adolescent initiation ceremonies could hardly be thought celebratory by unwilling or frightened participants.

The historical and cross-cultural relationships will be of considerable importance to a student undertaking work on any aspect of celebration. Connections and comparisons between different forms of ceremony and the reasons for their being will also be central considerations. Study of the theme should deal with more than superficial illustration; those decorations desired for a ritual, a festival such as Christmas, or a performance of an epic story like Ramayana. It will attempt to solve problems without cliché, make links without undue strain and be involved in serious critical appraisal of past and current interpretations. Perhaps for more than most projects the social, economic, political, religious and cultural context and implications will be of paramount importance. Research into these areas should enhance rather than encumber the excitement inherent in the theme. Its variety is considerable, as are the opportunities for creative work and intellectual involvement.

Above *Young Masai N'Dito in ceremonial dress*

Top right Adoration of the Kings. *Pieter Bruegel The Elder. 1598. Body colour on vellum. 32.9 × 47.9 cm. National Gallery, London*

Bottom right Laying a Foundation Stone. *L. S. Lowry. City Art Gallery, Manchester*

Areas of study

Celebration is:

Ritual	Party	Gala
Rite	Banquet	Fête
Pageant	Masquerade	Dance
Procession	Carnival	Festival
Cavalcade	Fair	Feast

Top left Les Plaisirs du Bal. *Antoine Watteau. Oil on canvas. 52.6 × 65.4 cm. Dulwich Picture Gallery, London*

Bottom left The Ball on Shipboard. *James Tissot. c. 1874. Oil on canvas. 84.1 × 129.5 cm. Tate Gallery, London*

Top right Temple decorations for a cremation celebration, Bali. 1986

Bottom right Snapshot of a birthday party

Celebration to:

Rejoice	Births, weddings, religious festivals, May Day.
Welcome	Return of sports winners to home town, Roman triumph, arrivals and returns.
Honour	Coronation, Lord Mayor's show, banquets.
Reward	Prize givings, sports days, presentations.
Commemorate	Anniversaries, jubilees, birthdays, American Thanksgiving, Chinese New Year, Saints' days, opening-bridges, roads, parliament, supermarkets,
Entertain	Parties, picnics, fun-fairs, sports events, circus, theatre, Comedia del Arte, masquerades, village fêtes, dances, carnivals.

In addition to the New York celebrations of different cultures projects could be based on some of the major religious festivals. For example:

Christian:

Advent – The days leading to Christmas.
Christmas – The birth of Christ.
Palm Sunday – Christ's entry into Jerusalem.
Easter – The ressurection of Christ.
Pentecost – The coming of the Holy Spirit.
Assumption – The taking up to heaven of the Virgin Mary.

Jewish:

Rosh Hashanah – New Year.
Hanukkah – Festival of Light.
Feast of the Passover – The celebration marking the Jews release from Egypt.
Pentecost – The coming of the Holy Spirit.
Purim – Women's festival.

Islamic:

'Eid al Fitr – The festival of fast-breaking which marks the end of Ramadan.
'Eid al-Adha (The Festival of Sacrifice) – The annual four day celebration which marks the completion of the *hajj*, that is the pilrimage to Mecca.

Hindu:

Lohri – Spring festival.
Hoi – The Festival of Colour.
Raksha bandhan (Rakhri) – The Festival of Sisters.
Dassehra – The celebration of Rama's Victory.
Diwalih Deepavali – The Festival of Light.

Sikh:

Tenth Guru Gobind Singh Ji's birthday.
Baisakhi – Birth of Sikhism.
Martyrdom of Guru Arjan Dev.
First Guru Nanak Dev Ji's birthday.
Martyrdom of Guru Tegh Bahadur Ji.
Three areas of celebration are outlined here, not as examples, but as indictors of how some aspects of the theme might be treated.

Weddings

The cross-cultural nature of this subject is obvious and there is opportunity in this country to study at first-hand the ceremonies of cultures other than our own, together with the numerous indigenous variations on the theme.

Research and practical work could be based on the following:

- The ways in which the visual aspects of the wedding ceremony are conditioned by cultural, religious, social, economic and climatic considerations.
- Comparative rituals i.e. the forms of the ceremony in different countries and at different times.
- Costume and organisational traditions e.g. dress and jewellery conventions, the type of celebration after the ceremony, the forms of eating and drinking, and the entertainment expected. Family and guest participation in feasting, singing and dancing, as well as in the actual ritual should not be overlooked.
- Portrayals of the ceremony i.e. how the event is recorded at the time by both professional and amateur means and possible later interpretations.

Such a project need not look only to the past or at present customs, but may involve the student in creative decisions about what might be desired by different people in future weddings, so bringing into play elements of design which would have to be decided upon in a real situation. For example:

- The design of invitations and other printed material.
- The design of the bride's dress, the accompanying accessories, the bridegroom's costume and that of the other major participants.
- The decoration of the place of the ceremony and reception.
- The design of the food and the layout and decoration of the tables.
- The type and organisation of the visual records e.g. photographs, film, video with possible later extensions into drawing and painting.
- The variety of entertainment to be provided and the amount of 'audience' participation expected and desired.

Above and right The Wedding of David and Ann in Hawaii 20 May 1983, © *David Hockney 1983. Photographic collage in three panels*

Left *Bridal group. Wedgewood. The Royal Pavilion, Art Gallery and Museums, Brighton*

Processions

A study of the different purposes of processions e.g. Processions for:

- The celebration of religious festivals e.g. Easter in Seville.
- Cremation in India and Indonesia, Chinese New Year.
- To honour someone e.g. the Lord Mayor's show, a coronation.
- To present an important personage e.g. Roman Triumph, Elizabethan Progress, the return of a successful sports team or personality.

The elements of popular art are evident here and these are portrayed in various media e.g. Mantegna's series of paintings at Hampton Court of the procession *The Triumph of Caesar* and press photographs and videos recording the return of successful FA Cup winners. Coronations, weddings, funeral corteges, protest and union marches, military and circus parades, pilgrimages, floral and village May Queen processions, May Day and numerous religious and state occassions are all part of the theme.

Needless to say the theme of processions is, with its elongated and sequential nature, most suitable for group work and other collaborative investigation.

73

Top Triumph of the Duchess Isabella van Alshoot. *Victoria and Albert Museum, London*

Far left *Chinese Dragon Dance. New Year Greeting Card. 1987*

Left *Mask of Rangda, Widow Witch, Goddess of Evil Spirits. Bali. 1985*

Above *Venetian carnival masks*

75

Carnival

Carnival, as we know it, has developed from what was originally considered as an activity which occurred on the festive days just prior to Lent, but it is obviously based on ancient festivals and forms of celebration. The name still evokes a scene of revelry and riot such as is depicted in Breughel's painting *The Contest Between Carnival and Lent* and seen in films and photographs of the famous carnivals in Rio de Janiero and Venice.

The subject is universal and many current and historical links and comparisons may be explored. For example:

- Medieval European carnivals and their association with the established church.
- Carnivals and fêtes related to saints' days.
- English spring festivals and village carnivals.
- Caribbean carnivals in this country e.g. Notting Hill, as well as in their country of origin.
- Nottingham Goose Fair.
- The Durham Miners' Gala.
- Chinese New Year celebrations.

The contextual implications are as important to study as the areas of costume, make-up, music, dance and decoration. The subject raises serious social issues related to repression, religion, politics, economics and status; consideration of which is essential for an intelligent appreciation; without which the project might be but superficial.

Left Mother's Day Out. *Grace Robertson. Courtesy of the photographer*

Below Masqueraders of the Cross River, *Nigeria. Horniman Museum, London*

Drawing

Themes for projects need not be limited to a subject or a concept base. A practice or working method may be taken and is just as educationally valuable. Although drawing is used here as an example, other practices such as painting, carving and knitting could also be themes. Most teachers of art and design recognise the importance of drawing and often emphasise it to their students by making it the starting point, if not the core, of what is done. It is considered to be a key part of art and design, a basic skill without which the visual development of ideas is limited. Yet often the interpretation of drawing is itself limited, the range of its uses narrow, and the approach expected and encouraged confined to the Western European fine art tradition.

Without doubt some of the requirements of the previous examinations have been responsible for this approach and it is to be hoped that these will not be carried over to restrict the broader educational intentions of the new examination. Projects related to drawing might be made more varied by encouraging research into the different uses of the practice, rather than by concentrating on the acquisition of skill which is based on notions of Renaissance perspective. Is there a sound educational reason for excluding from the student's experience those forms of drawing which do not deal with optical illusions? But this is the theme of another project.

Areas of study

Whilst the sections listed below are possible areas of study for projects and each part of them could be the topic for a more detailed investigation, variations related to the interests of individual students might be made by combining together aspects from each section. For example, drawing for the communication of information might include a consideration of some of the following:

- Renaissance pattern books;
- contemporary illustration relating to recognition e.g. books of ships, aeroplanes, cars, birds, plants and flowers;
- projections and diagrams in instruction manuals;
- botanical illustration;
- maps and plans;
- linear representation in pencil, pen and print.

Top left Warrior head-dress. 1986.
Children's design. Tabernacle carnival club

Top right Inca and headhunter.
Designer Lawrence Noel. Trinbago
carnival club

Bottom Cremation Ceremony, Bali. 1985

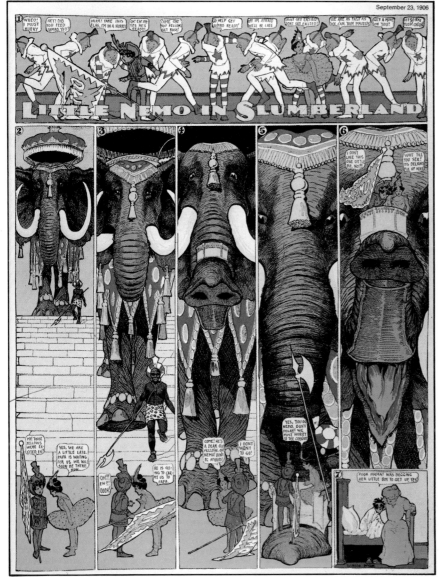

Top left Omina. *Designer Vernon Williams. Genesis. Notting Hill Carnival Queen 1985*

Top right Cocoyea magic. *Designer Frank Alexander. Design in Mind. Notting Hill Carnival Queen 1986*

Bottom Little Nemo in Slumberland. *Windsor McCay. 23 September 1906*

Top left Reclining Figure. *Sam Rabin. 1949. Biro on paper. 30.1 × 54.9 cm. Dulwich Picture Gallery, London*

Bottom left Giant Squid. *Victorian reportage drawing*

Bottom right Man with Hat. *Georges Seurat. Conté crayon. British Museum, London*

The student would thus learn about:

- a practice – drawing for the communication of information in a number of media.
- a basic element of art and design – line (and shape);
- a working process – project-based thematic enquiry which might also include: sequential study, discussion and critical appraisal, and would certainly involve visual research, observation and analysis.

Some purposes of drawing

- For the collection of information i.e. recording
- For the communication of information
- For analysis
- For exploring ideas
- For expressing ideas and emotions
- As synthesis
- To indicate space
- To create an illusion of space
- To indicate the third dimension
- To create an illusion of the third dimension
- To decorate
- For an understanding of the subject being drawn

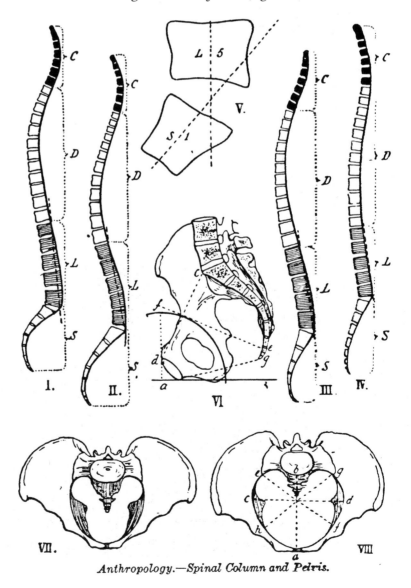

Right Anatomical drawing

Anthropology.—Spinal Column and Pelvis.

Top left Reclining Figure. *Henry Moore. 1974. Charcoal, pastel and watercolour. 22.7 × 35.2 cm. Henry Moore Foundation*

Top right Sketchbook drawing for a painting. *Edgar Blakeney. c. 1954. Pencil on paper with pen colour notes. 33.0 × 25.4 cm*

Bottom left A Garden at St Remy. *Vincent van Gogh. 1899. Pen and ink, pencil and chalk. 62.3 × 48.0 cm. Tate Gallery, London*

Bottom centre White Heron among Lotuses. *Buncho. Oriental Museum, University of Durham*

Bottom right Exploded drawing. *Pen and ink.*

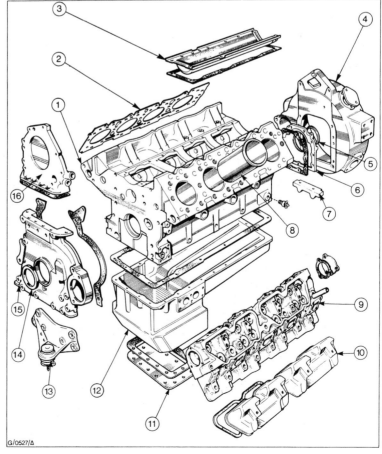

G/0527/Δ

Top left *Man and woman. Blown-up detail of an engraving:* The Combat. *G. T. Doo after a painting by William Etty, R.A. 1848. 28.6 × 38.1 cm. Collection Dr Anthony Dyson*

Top right *Fantaisie sur le costume moderne. Leon Baxst. 1912. Whereabouts unknown.*

Bottom left *Santa Maria della Spina, Pisa. John Ruskin. 1845. Watercolour. 50.2 × 37.8 cm. Ruskin Gallery, Sheffield*

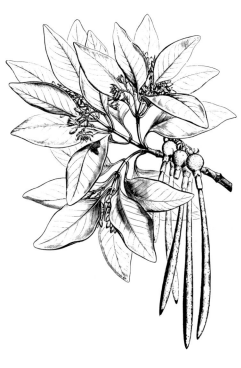

Some types of drawing

- Objective
- Non-figurative
- Topographical
- Architectural
- Botanical illustration
- Medical illustration
- Story illustration
- Cartographic
- Charts, diagrams and graphs
- Technical
- Fashion
- Pattern design
- Reportage
- Idea sketches
- Drawing systems e.g. mathematical perspective, exploded drawings, simultaneous viewpoint, isometric projection, oblique projection, axonometric projection.

Above *Botanical illustration*

Right Nature morte. *Pierre Bonnard. 1922. Pencil. Collection Alfred Ayrton*

PATIENCE REWARDED.

Piscator. "A-HAH! GOT YOU AT LAST, HAVE I?—AND A FINE WEEK'S TROUBLE I'VE HAD TO CATCH YOU!"

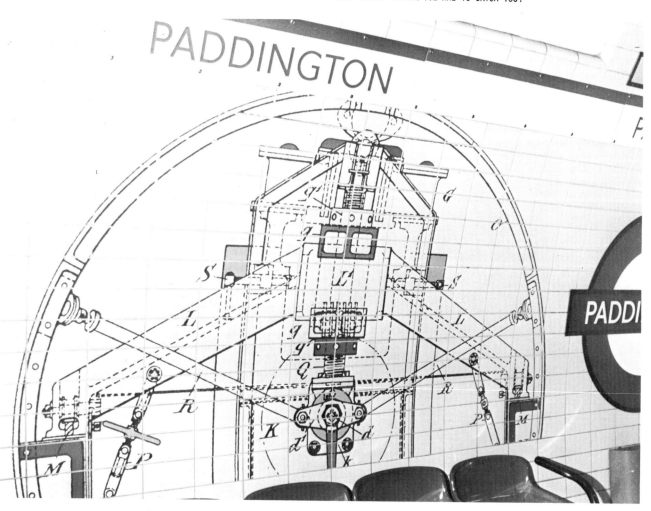

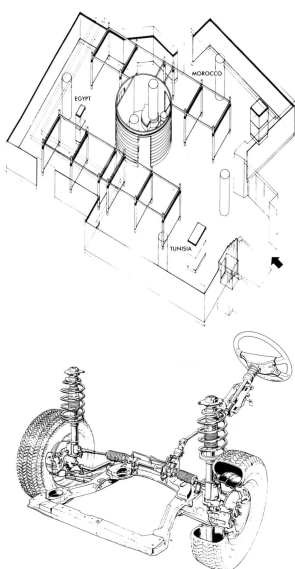

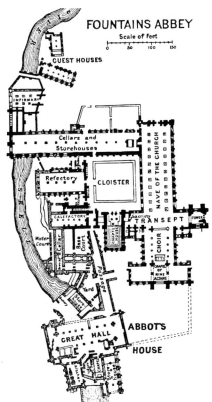

FOUNTAINS ABBEY

Scale of Feet

0   50   100   150

GUEST HOUSES

INFIRMARY

Cellars and
Storehouses

NAVE OF THE CHURCH

Refectory

CLOISTER

CALEFACTORY

TRANSEPT

TOWER

Water
Court

CHOIR

CHAPEL
OF
NINE
ALTARS

GREAT HALL

ABBOTS
HOUSE

Top left *Cartoon by John Leech. c. 1850.*
Pen and ink.

Bottom left *Enlarged engineering drawing*
on to tiles of a London Underground Station
from an original by Isambard Kingdom
Brunel

This page *Diagrams*

Drawing media

- Pencil
- Colour crayon, chalk, pastel, oil pastel
- Pen and ink, reed, bamboo, quill etc.
- Brush and wash
- Airbrush
- Cut line: lino, woodcut, etching, engraving
- Print: block, silkscreen on paper or fabric
- Batik
- Ceramic glaze
- Scissors and knives e.g. paper cut-outs, papier collé by Matisse.
- Three-dimensional drawing with paper, card, wire, thread etc.

Elements

- Line
- Shape
- Pattern
- Texture
- Colour
- Tone
- Form

Drawing as a means of indicating space

Below Two Samurai. Japanese woodcut. Nineteenth century.

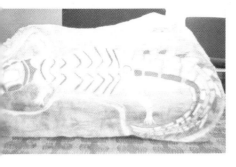

Above Crocodile. Australian aborigial painting. Coloured earth and orchid juice on tree bark. c. 50 cm. St Aidan's College, Durham

Right Whirling Log. Navaho Indian 1966. Sandpainting. Diameter 1.75 m. Horniman Museum London

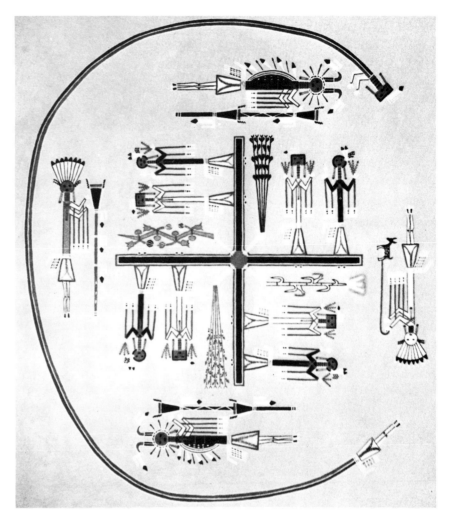

1 By the position of forms on the picture-plane i.e. one above another.
2 By overlapping forms.
3 By varying the scale of forms.
4 By the use of colour and tone.
5 By linear perspective: one point, two points, three points and exaggerated perspective.
6 By employing one or more projection system e.g. oblique, isometric.
7 By the use of multiple viewpoints combined on the one surface.

Each of the areas of study above could be used as the theme for a project either singly or in conjunction with others. Although on first reading they might appear to be based on two-dimensional representation, there is no reason why some of these notions may not be used in three-dimensional construction, for non-figurative work and as part of a design process.

Drawing and pictorial composition

For example:
■ Grids, modules, tessellations.
■ Mathematical devices in Western European painting; the Golden Section, the Fibonacci Series, Le Corbusier's Modular.
■ Non-European structural devices; Tantra, Japanese Tatami mat units, North American Chilcut blanket design, totem pole organisation and sand drawings.
■ Folk art e.g. Polish and Chinese paper cut-outs, Indonesian batik and shadow puppets.

89

Top left *Paper cut-out. China. Mid twentieth century. 26.7 × 16.5 cm*

Bottom left *Computer graphic design. Richard Colson. 1987. Image produced on the Quantel Paintbox and photographed at BPCC Videographics on the DAI Nippon Image Recorder*

Above *Fan. Assam, India. Nineteenth century. Peacock feathers and porcupine quills. Victoria and Albert Museum, London*

Pattern and Texture

Surfaces intrigue. They arouse our desire to touch, reflect our need to organise. They are what we choose to wear, what we decorate our surroundings with, and what we confront all our waking hours. They are perhaps more obvious in design than in painting, more an integral part of craft than art, but nonetheless, surface is a consideration in painting and sculpture. Is the texture of a subject represented with near verisimiltude as in a painting by Willem Kalf with polished silver, shiny horn, rough pile of carpet or is it suggested as in a Wilson Steer beachscape? Perhaps the texture of the subject is one with the texture of paint as in a meadow painted by Van Gogh. Or are we meant to respond to the texture of paint as used by Chaim Soutine, an Impressionist or Abstract Expressionist? How is texture used by sculptors? Are we asked to respond to the material texture of stone, wood, marble, wax, plaster, clay or is conflict aroused by unusual and unexpected uses of material as in *Present* (a flat iron with

Above *Pottery jug slipware, the head detachable to form a cup. Eighteenth century. Staffordshire, England. Height 22.3 cm. Fitzwilliam Museum, Cambridge*

Right *Bird and Flower Dado. Jeffrey and Co. 1880. Whitworth Art Gallery, University of Manchester*

91

tin tacks stuck on it) by Man Ray, *Fur Cup, Saucer and Spoon* by Meret Oppenheim or the soft sculptures of the American Claes Oldenburg? Is pattern both two and three-dimensional in painting, sculpture, photography and architecture?

Surface in terms of pattern and texture is a basic element of art and design and any investigation of it should include a serious consideration of the design aspect. We need to look at historical pattern books, wallpaper, fabric design, plastering, pargetting and furniture as well as those crafts such as weaving, knitting, needlecraft, lace, crochet, basket and cane-work.

Areas of study

- Pattern as visual composition e.g. the organisation in paintings by Piero della Francesca, Fra Angelico, Paul Cézanne, Georges Seurat.
- The visual 'rhymes' and repetitions in the work of such painters as Nicholas Poussin, Henri Matisse, Pablo Picasso.

Pattern

Intentional

- Those patterns in **nature** which are functional, such as the skins, pelts, hides and plumage of creatures which are designed to attract or disguise.
- Those patterns which **man makes** for the same purpose or to package, stack, organise and arrange in some manner.

Left Patterned shopfront – intentional pattern

Below Lupin seedpods – natural functional pattern

Above *Shadows – accidental pattern*

Unintentional

A grouping of identical or similar units which occur accidentally or are placed in an arrangement governed by non-visual considerations. e.g. fallen leaves, confetti, heaped peas, pulses, pasta, books on shelves, traffic, parked cars, footprints in sand and snow.

These two basic, broad categories may be broken down into more specific ones.

■ **Natural** In nature most pattern is functional, even that which is decorative; pattern to attract or disguise, pattern as structure e.g. the 'packaging' of seeds, the growth forms of plants, habitat structures such as honeycombs. Natural and non-functional instances of patterning occur in cases of weathering, decay, erosion, strata faults and the movement of water.

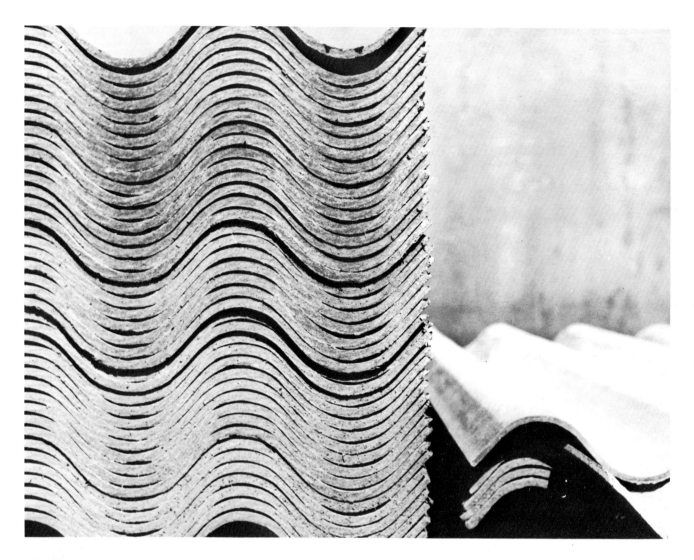

■ **Man-made** Both structural and decorative patterns are made by man and not always in conjunction. A printed fabric may have a design unrelated to its structure, whereas a knitted or woven textile will have the pattern of the knit or weave which is structural and may have, as in the case of an Aran sweater, a decorative element which is integral with the structure. (The decoration is also functional as it was originally designed for family identification.)

■ **Regular** People's desire to organise is strong and we tend to work towards symmetry and a certain amount of repetition. This is particularly so in the case of functional items e.g. stacked bricks, wood, chairs, and other items of similar unit shape: tins, boxes, packets. This tendency is less obvious in the case of things which are purely decorative or visual.

■ **Irregular** Most man-made coincidental patterns are irregular. The items listed in the preceding paragraph could as easily be found in irregular formations. Natural irregularity is often intentional e.g. animal and insect camouflage, but can occur by chance e.g. fallen leaves.

■ **Functional and decorative** In addition to the few simple examples listed above, it may be worth considering some of the patterns created by modern technology e.g. computer images and printouts, telex tapes, punched cards, braille and electronic circuits. In this context the calligraphy and printing of various cultures could be included.

Above Stacked corrugated sheets – man-made functional pattern

94

Above *Reflections – natural irregular pattern*

Right *Buildings – man-made, regular, structural pattern*

Texture

Texture may be broken down into study areas similar to those suggested for pattern, but in addition the inherent qualities will need to be recognised.

Pattern and texture are sometimes confused, which is not surprising for there are instances when each presents elements of the other. In their investigation of surfaces students may need clarification and help in understanding that visual pattern is the repetition of identical

or similar lines, shapes, forms or colours, whilst texture is the tactile quality of a surface, its roughness or smoothness.

Tactile texture

Those surfaces which may be appreciated both by touch and sight. The sensations received by the two senses may not always be the same e.g. a snake skin.

Top left Natural pattern and texture

Top right Wooden door – natural and man-made pattern and texture

Bottom Natural tactile texture

Above *Close-up of a poster – man-made optical texture*

Optical texture

There are surfaces which, although appearing to have a pronounced tactile quality have in fact little e.g. polished wood, cork or tile, veined marble, speckled eggs, smooth pebbles, printed papers and fabrics. Our appreciation of such textures is visual. Added to this category may be those textures which although having a definite 'surface' quality can, because of size, composition or distance only be appreciated optically e.g. a landscape, a mountain, trees, the facade of a building, a painting or sculpture.

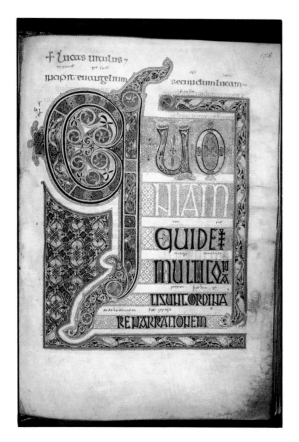

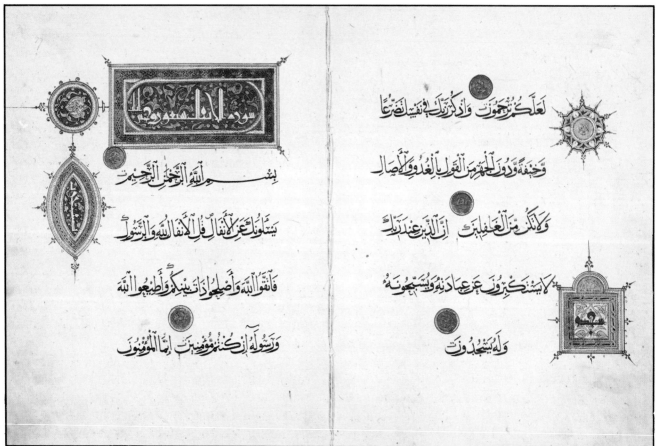

Top left *The Lindisfarne Gospels. Opening page of St Luke's Gospel. British Library*

Top right *Lindisfarne decorated cross-carpet page preceeding St Luke. British Library*

Bottom *Koran. Surah VIII verses 1–3. Egypt. Fourteenth century. British Library*

Right *Frontispiece from a Mamluk Koran. Egypt. Fourteenth century. British Library*

98

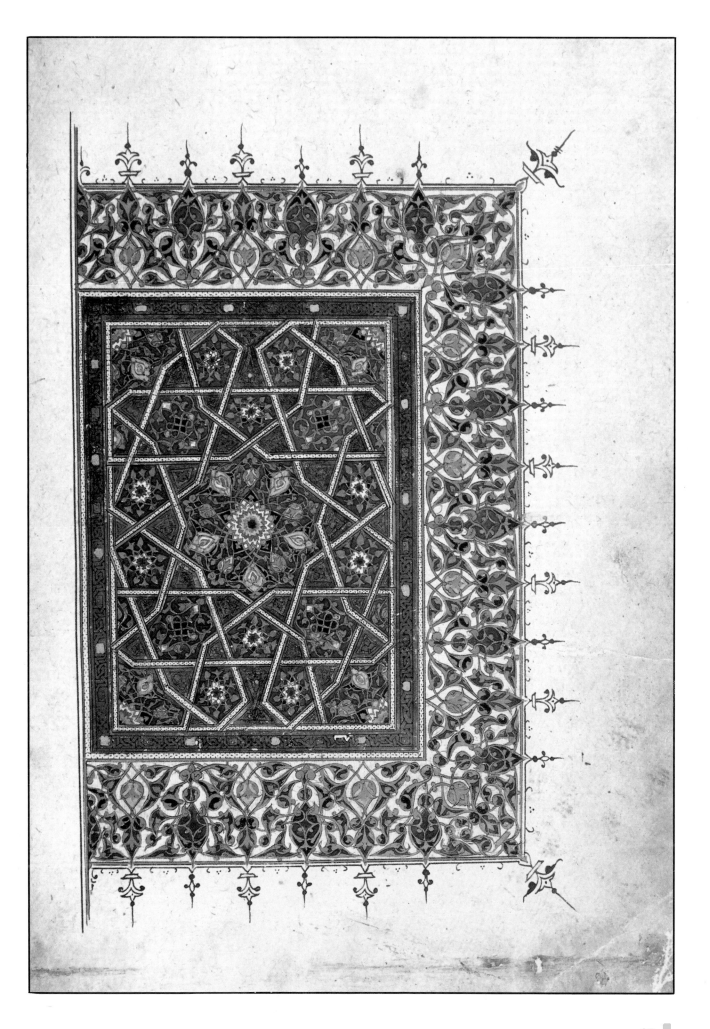

Ephemeral texture

Some textures alter as we watch or touch them, are in a constant state of change, or by nature are temporary e.g. sea foam, soap bubbles, oil on water, rain on windowpanes, frost and snow.

Above Bracelet armpiece. Caroline Broadhead. Crafts Council

Left Close-up of a painting in a raking light

100

Top left *Trees*

Top right *Beachscene*

Bottom right Birds. *Tapestry. 1.85 ×
1.58 m. Wissa Wassef Art School, Cairo*

Left *Iznik tiles from the facade of the Rüstem Pasa Mosque, Istanbul. Photograph by Dr Ahmet Ertug/Zamana Gallery, London*

Above Group of Dancers. *Edgar Degas. National Gallery of Scotland.*

104

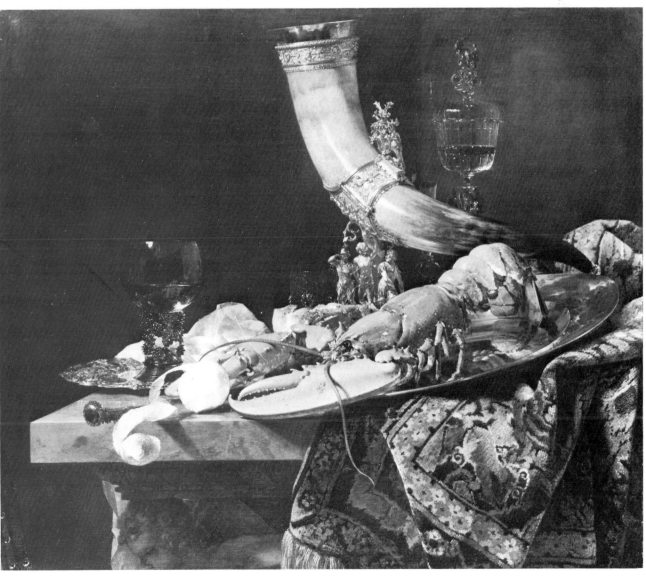

Structure

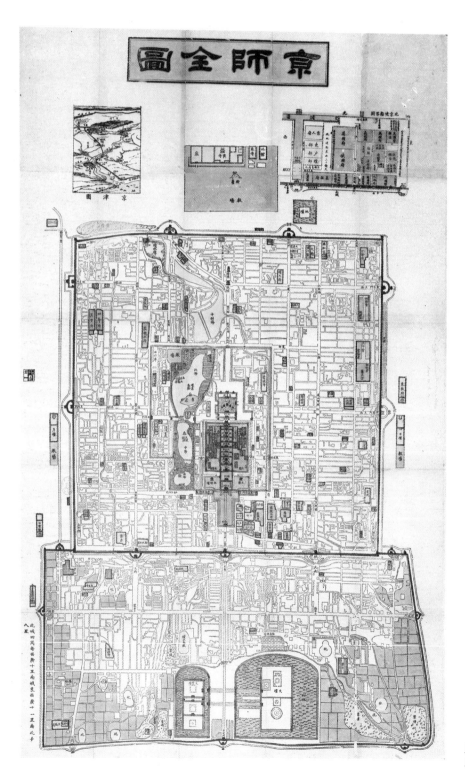

Left Map of Peking. Woodcut. British Library

Top right *Christmas Crib. Cracow, Poland. 1955. Height 1.45 m. Horniman Museum, London*

Bottom right Ice Scupture. *Scour Water, Dumfriesshire. January 1987. Andy Goldsworthy*

Structure here refers to three-dimensional objects which have been built, their separate pieces fitted together to make a whole (from the Latin *struo*, to build). Many art and design courses are, at present, planned so that the student's experience moves from the second to the third-dimension. Drawings develop either into paintings, two-dimensional graphic designs and prints with possible extensions into some area of construction, or else through plans and variations to the manufacture of a design product. Although this is not exclusively the procedure it is a common pattern. Pottery is often a notable exception. The practical difficulties encountered when dealing with materials and organisation for work in the third-dimension can make it a neglected area of study, particularly in those small departments with limited facilities or experience. It is simpler and safer to remain with two-dimensions.

Such an attitude though understandable is odd. Our experience as very young children is certainly visual but it is also extremely tactile. For a child, the physical act of making a mark on a flat surface is a three-dimensional experience. The holding of the implement, the encounter with the 'picture-plane', and the movement through space are all a form of construction; the act as much as the resulting mark.

Top left Paddy fields near Tirtagangga, Bali

Bottom left Iron crosses and plant

Above Ice scupture. *Scour Water, Dumfresshire. January 1987. Andy Goldsworthy*

After such early experiences as modelling food, drawing with drinks, stretching, pushing, tearing and assembling anything within reach, and later having these delights formalised with sand and water play, and the equipment of the primary school, our experience becomes somewhat less spatial and our education less physical.

There is, of course, no right or wrong way of organising three-dimensional work in relationship to other aspects of the art and design curriculum. To insist on a sound understanding of two-dimensional work before constructional activities can begin is as limiting as the reverse notion. Drawing may be an acknowledged basis of all we do, but that does not mean that the student's initial involvement in a project may not be to 'draw' in the third-dimension. Perhaps direct involvement with materials and structural concepts will help to maintain early excitement and enthusiasm, and rekindle a sense of wonder.

Areas of study

The inter-relationship between the areas of study listed below is obvious and many links and selections are possible which may be used in conjunction with other projects where a structural component is desirable. Each of the areas listed may be a part of a project or the project theme itself.

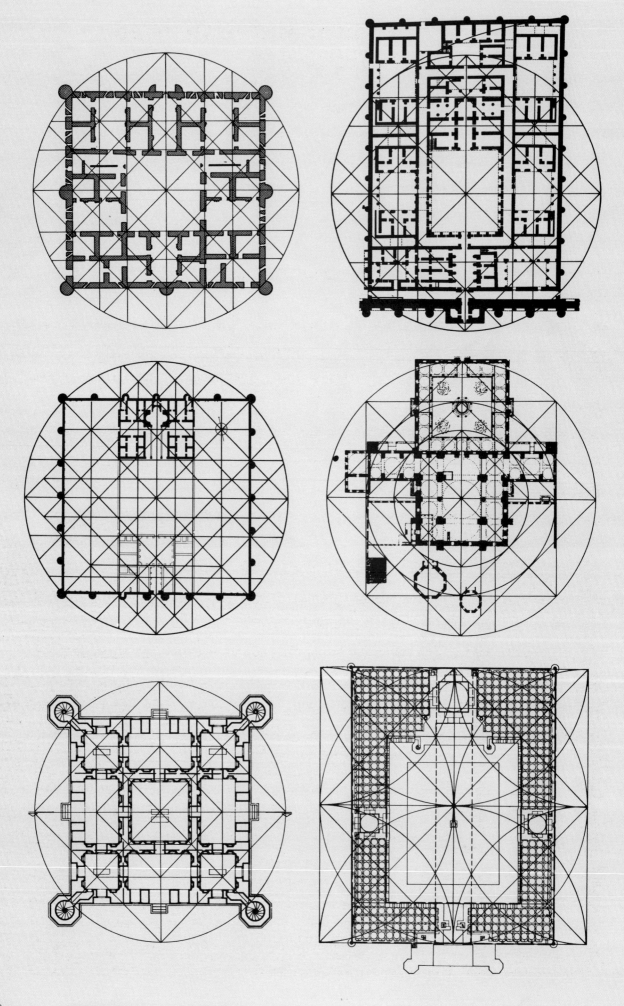

Natural and man-made structures

Functional

Environmental organisation	ant hill – shopping precinct
Spaces for living	wasps nest – block of flats
Load bearing	bone – chair
Spanning	spider's web – bridge
Storing	honey comb – shelving
Packaging	egg – egg box
Transporting	sycamore seeds – helicopter
Covering	snail shell – clothing

Non-functional

It may be argued that in nature there is no such thing as a non-functional structure, all natural forms having a purpose. Some man-made structures are both functional and decorative, for example, load-bearing sculptures as part of architecture, but we also build for pleasure, to express ideas and feelings and to evoke responses from other people. In addition to different forms of sculpture and assemblage there are objects made for decorating ourselves, our homes and our possessions, for example, jewellery, glass and porcelain figurines, car badges, mascots and souvenirs. There are also decorative objects made in the form of functional ones, for example, commemorative plates, bowls and silver cups.

Constructional considerations

- Space – penetration and enclosure
- Length, height, width and weight
- Balance
- Unit repetition
- Movement – mechanical, for example, motorised machine, kinetic sculpture
  non-mechanical, for example, mobiles
  static expression, for example, modelled, carved and assembled sculpture
- Appropriateness of materials and tools
- Appropriateness of constructional process e.g. modelling, construction, carving, casting, assemblage, soft sculpture
- The relationship of the construction to its purpose and/or setting e.g. interior, exterior, religious, ritualistic, festive, practical, illustrative, evocative, instructional

Top right *Eiffel tower and trees, Paris*

Bottom right *Font Cover. South Acre Church, Norfolk*

Left *Temple decorations made from bamboo and palm leaves. Indonesia. 1986*

Basic concepts

Three-dimensional structures penetrate space i.e. displace, and may at the same time enclose space. For example, a sculptured head by Giacometti may penetrate space, a sculpted form by Moore enclose (and perforce displace), whilst a chair may both penetrate and enclose in a more obvious manner.

112

Top right Old Walton Bridge. *Antonio Canaletto. 1754. Oil on canvas. 48.8 × 76.7 cm. Dulwich Picture Gallery, London*

Bottom right The Cutty Sark, *Greenwich, London*

Below Han Tower. *Second century* BC *China. Ceramic. British Museum*

Research into forms which penetrate space may include aspects of extending, expanding, piercing, spreading, twisting, turning.

Research into forms which enclose space may include aspects of encircling, covering, surrounding, wrapping, twisting.

Constructional activities

Emphasis will need to be placed on the desired outcome and the relevance of tools and materials to the structure.

- **Dividing** by cutting, splitting, tearing, piercing, slicing, sawing.
- **Joining** by assembling, grouping, piling, layering, jointing, sticking, slotting, nailing, screwing, pining, weaving.
- **Supporting** by propping, bracing, hanging, suspending, buttressing.

113

Possible development

1 Identification of the problem

- What exactly has been requested by the teacher or what has been the required aim decided by the student?
- Who will benefit from the result? Who is the final structure aimed at? What is its purpose?
- In what situation will the production be used or presented?
- Are there ergonomic, social, financial, political, functional, or celebratory factors involved?
- Make a checklist of requirements.

2 Investigation

- Location, consumer, library, picture, historical and cultural research.
- Consideration of possible solutions in the light of solutions in other times and cultures to similar problems.

3 Solution

- Sketches, working drawings and models as appropriate and in whichever order is decided.
- A consideration of size, time, cost and those items listed in the section on constructional activities above.
- Selection of suitable materials, tools and facilities.
- Application of relevant skills.
- Decision on the way forward.

Left The Virgin and Child Enthroned with Scenes of the Nativity and Lives of the Saints. *Margarito of Arezzo. Active 1262. Oil on wood. National Gallery, London. (See page 124.)*

Right Michelir. *Advertising series. (See page 124.)*

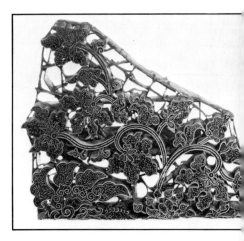

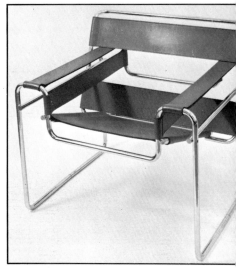

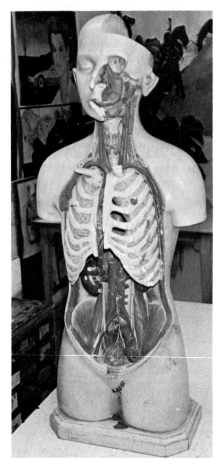

4 Realisation

■ Final selection for the most appropriate means of resolution.
■ Identification of particular constructional problems.
■ Decision on the order of progress i.e. consolidation of last session.
■ Construction and realisation.

5 Evaluation

■ Have all aspects of the brief been dealt with?
■ Check the original check list!
■ By what means can a decision be made as to whether or not the solution is successful?
■ Apply those means.
■ Spectator/consumer testing – by what method?
■ Decide and apply methods.
■ Analysis of the problems encountered, both those forseen and unforseen. What were the solutions? Did they work?
■ Research into audience/consumer reaction.
■ Suggestions for modification and/or improvement of both the intention and the outcome.

Top left Wall of the Mosque, Cordoba, Spain

Top right Batik Stamp. Bali. Metal. 21 × 26 cm. Private collection

Centre right Wassily Chair. Marcel Bruer. 1902. Sainsbury Centre for Visual Arts, Norwich

Bottom left Toy bicycle. Zimbabwe teenager. c. 1980. Wire. Length 25 cm Horniman Museum, London

Bottom right Medical model

Below Human skull with pearl shell decoration, used in divination. Torres Straits. Length 20 cm. Museum of Mankind, London

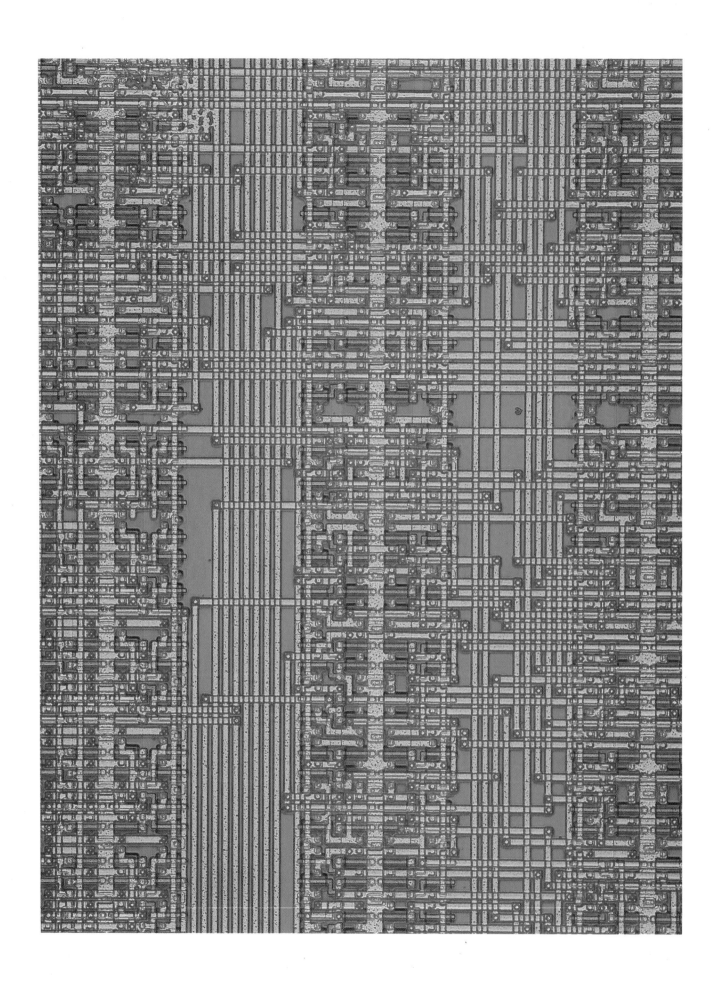

Above *Light micrograph of part of the surface of a 16K 4116 memory integrated circuit (silicon chip), a type of memory chip commonly used in printed circuit boards*

Above *Little Nemo in Slumberland. Windsor McCay. 29 October 1905. (See page 124.)*

Top left and right Stairs 4. Rein Jansma. 1982. Cut and folded paper, 38 × 57 cm

Centre, bottom left and right Animals. Lygia Clark. Sainsbury Centre for Visual Arts, Norwich

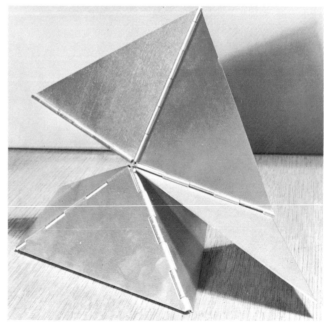

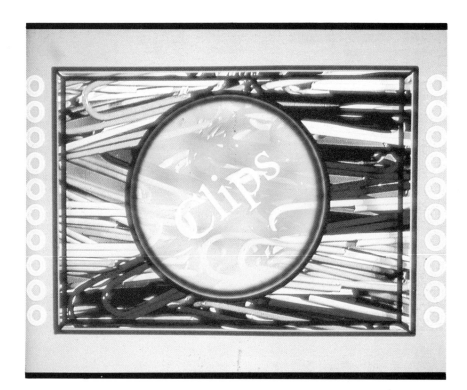

Top right *Computer image by Richard Colson. 1987. Image produced on the Quantel Paintbox and photographed at BPCC Videographics on the DAI Nippon Image Recorder*

Bottom left and right *Isphahan tiles and diagrams. Photo by Alistair Duncan*

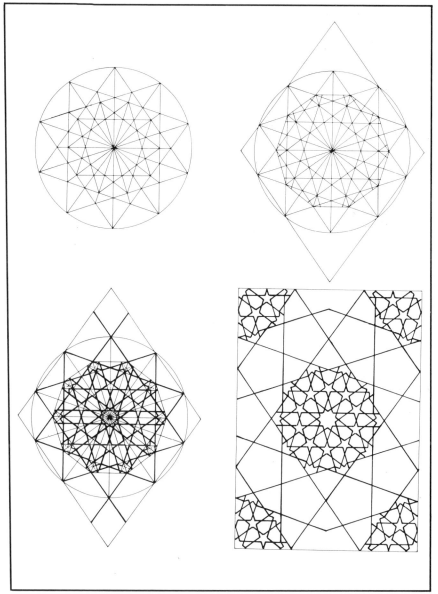

Above Girls Swimming in a Lotus Pool. *Pahari School Garhwal, India. c. 1790.*
British Museum, London. (See page 135.)

WHERE DO THEY GET THEIR ENERGY?

Running. Jumping. Chasing the cat. Growing kids seldom stand still.

But then we should be thankful for small mercies. Because an energetic child is invariably a healthy child, too.

Kids don't just need energy for dashing about. They actually need energy to help them grow.

And that's where milk comes in. It's one of the major sources of energy in a child's diet.

And since it's so near to hand in the fridge, they can get it whenever they need it. So they can carry on performing those death-defying cartwheels in double-quick time.

AS WELL AS ENERGY, MILK PROVIDES ESSENTIAL CALCIUM, PROTEIN AND VITAMINS

Milk is also the major natural source of calcium in a child's diet. A pint a day will provide them with all the calcium they need to build and maintain strong, healthy teeth and bones.

It will also provide them with other

WHAT A PINT OF MILK PROVIDES	PASTEURISED	HOMO-GENISED	CHANNEL ISLANDS	SEMI-SKIMMED	SKIMMED	STERILISED
Calcium	702mg	702mg	702mg	729mg	761mg	702mg
Calories (Energy)	380	380	445	280	195	380
Total Fat	22.2g (3.8%)	22.2g (3.8%)	28.1g (4.8%)	10.5g (1.8%)	0.6g (0.1%)	22.2g (3.8%)
Protein	19.3g	19.3g	21.1g	19.5g	19.9g	19.3g
Carbohydrate (Lactose)	27.5g	27.5g	27.5g	28.4g	29.3g	27.5g
SOURCE: McCance and Widdowson's 'The Composition of Foods' 1978.						

essential components they need to grow strong and healthy.

Protein, to build and repair their bodies' cells. Carbohydrate, again, for energy.

And vitamins like A, B_1, B_2 and B_{12}, for healthy eyes, skin, gums and blood formation.

IT'S ONE HABIT YOU SHOULD ENCOURAGE

Doctors recommend they have whole milk, at least until the age of five, because it provides more energy than skimmed or semi-skimmed milks.

But because milk is the most complete food there is, even if they choose skimmed or semi-skimmed when they're older, you can be sure they'll still be getting the essential goodness that all kinds of milk provide.

To help ensure they stay bouncing with health.

Everybody's body needs bottle

Above Milk advertisement. (See page 135.)

Series, Serial and Sequence

When we consider the images which are created for visual communication we generally think of single images, a drawing or painting, a print, a photograph, a piece of sculpture. However, this is not always the case. We may remember a scene from a play, a sequence from a film, or a television programme. Even when in the studio, we make a number of studies or preparatory drawings, sketch out ideas or break down a technical process into a logical sequence, we concern ourselves with the end product, the final version towards which we have been working.

We often regard the works in galleries and museums in terms of individual items and yet in reality they relate to each other, to their setting, the decor and furnishings which surround them, and of course to visitors other than ourselves, all of which we see and which have some effect upon our appreciation and understanding.

Whenever we look around us we juxtopose images. The eye moves from one view to another. Each day is a visual sequence and the notion of related images is well worth exploring both in terms of understanding and creating.

Areas of Study

Series

A series is a variation on a theme. It is usually a collection of a number of single moments in time. In the school art room this often happens accidentally. A number of paintings of a particular subject are produced, the still life is available, the stuffed animal or costume has been hired and must be used to the maximum effect before the return date. However, a series with a particular purpose can be planned so that there is every chance that interest will be maintained and an educational objective achieved. Painters do not produce a series of works by default. There may be an initial enthusiasm for the subject, but there is usually an idea which requires development, a thought which the artist wishes to explore.

With this in mind it might be possible to argue that an artist returning time and again to a particular motif, or idea, is producing an extended series. Are all the paintings of Mte. Ste. Victoire by Cézanne a series, or is the fact that they were produced over many

Boxers. Sam Rabin

Top The Last Round. *Wax crayon on paper. 37.0 × 49.8 cm*

Bottom Boxing Match II. *Wax crayon on board. 25.8 × 30.7 cm*

124

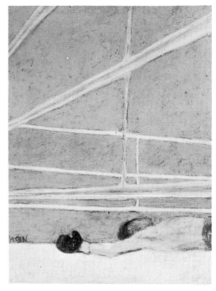

Top left Boxing Match I. *Wax crayon on board. 72.6 × 99.5 cm*

Top right Knockout. *Wax crayon on board. 49.0 × 37.5 cm*

Bottom left Tense Moment Study. *Wax crayon on board. 22.4 × 15.7 cm*

Bottom right The Prelude. *Wax crayon on board. 56.4 × 50.1 cm*

Left Screw Mobile. *Kenneth Martin.*
Copper and bronze. (See page 135.)

This page *Chahkobi (tea serving doll)*
with and without costume. Courtesy of The
Japan Foundation. (See page 135.)

years contrary to that thought? The relationship between series and time is worth exploring for there is no doubt that the conclusions reached will vary with the artists discussed. Examples of series may be found in television, advertising images, newspapers and magazines.

Series may be considered as a number of variations of an idea or subject which interests the artist, or interpretations of work by other painters, sculptors and designers. The first category could include, as well as the obvious figure, landscape and flower subjects, those incidents from myth, legend and religion which are such an important part of the art of most cultures. A comparative study of the ways in which different people have portrayed events from the life of Christ at different times need not be confined to Western European art but could consider the work of African, Russian and Far Eastern artists. Popular art would be an integral part of such a study. A similar approach might look at the life of Krishna or other gods, goddesses, heroes and heroines from all over the world.

The second category, whilst perhaps dealing with some of the above, might also contain thematic interpretations across the arts as well as the more familiar variations by one artist on the work of another. For example:

- Pablo Picasso's variations on Manet's *Le Déjeuner sur l'herbe* which was itself a variation on a detail of Marcantonio's engraving after Raphael's *Judgement of Paris* and a direct relative of Giorgione's *Concert Champêtre*.
- Van Gogh's paintings of Japanese prints.
- Ceri Richard's extended series inspired by the piano piece *La Cathedrale Engloutie* by Claude Debussy.
- Richard Hamilton's *Interior* paintings, assemblages and prints derived from a still from the film *Shockproof*.

Variations on the themes of artists are not confined to other artists but can form the basis for fashion, jewellery and textile design as well as appearing in film, television, architecture and advertising.

A simple introduction to the theme could be for students to make drawings and paintings of a still life which show different aspects and viewpoints e.g.

1 Painted in pure colour.
2 Painted in shades of one colour.
3 Painted with different light sources.
4 Drawn from low and high viewpoints.
5 Drawn from long shot to close-up or vice versa. (Which might develop into a serial or a sequence.)

A number of working drawings and designs might be variations of ideas rather than a progression towards a resolution. Also, prints, perhaps in different colour-ways, and maquettes and constructions which show different interpretations of a subject or alternative solutions to a problem.

Above Escape of a Zebra from the Zoo. *Carel Weight. City Art Gallery, Manchester*

Serial

Serial relates to time. It is a diary, a development of related episodes or moments. Serial is about a progression, about differences which are linked but which do not necessarily culminate in a final statement. There is also the possibility of continuation if the creator so desires. We see this in television and also in advertising. Many newspaper cartoons are examples of serials as are some magazine stories and, of course, there are many examples in painting and print making. For example:

- Giotto – *The Life of S. Francis* (Assisi)
- Giotto – *The Life of Christ* (Padua)
- Monet – *Rouen Cathedral*
- Monet – *Haystacks*
- Monet – *Waterlilies*
- Monet – *Poplars*
- Henry Moore – Sheep drawings
- William Hogarth – *The Rake's Progress, Marriage ā la Mode*
- David Hockney – *The Rake's Progress*

The notion of progression might be introduced by an examination of those paintings by Piet Mondrian which show an abstracting from the visible world towards a non-figurative image. For example, *The Apple Tree* (1911–12), *Facades, Ginger Pot* (1912). The series of bas relief figures *The Back* which Matisse made between 1909 and 1930 is another instance of such an approach. The area of book and story illustration is also important and early film serials could also be considered.

Project work on the theme of serial might include a serial record or interpretation of a period of time: a day, a walk, the seasons, decay, the progression of an event such as a meal or a procession, the movements of someone at work or play, and, as with Impressionism, the changes of light and the weather.

Interpretations of serial activities such as movement which may relate to photography (and the work of the early experimenters), film, video and comic strips as well as the work of the Futurists may also involve extensions of a different kind. For example, the selection of a painting and creation of not only a variation, but also a depiction of what happened before and after the event shown; or a representation of the action from a number of differing viewpoints. A work with a strong dramatic content such as the *Battle of San Romano* by Paul Uccello might be a good one to take, but alternatively the idea could be used with a quiet interior by Vermeer, or a completely non-figurative picture. Such a project could easily extend into sequence.

The design process itself is a form of serial, progressing from initial sketches through drawings, prototypes, colour ways, test pieces and models to a final realisation.

A design application of the notion of serial might be made by the production of a visual explanation, either realistically or diagramatically, of a process (e.g. textile designing and printing), an assembly (e.g. a car maintenance manual), a mechanical function (e.g. an industrial production process) or may show the stages of development related to a long term project (e.g. urban expansion). The concept of serial vision; that is, the production of a number of images which move from long shot to a close-up of detail, or vice versa, to place the detail in context might be incorporated into the design application or be used as the subject of the project itself.

Sequence

A visual sequence is an organised set of images, each one of which relates to the others. Each image is specifically linked to those placed immediately before and after and is essential to an appreciation and understanding of the whole.

Some of the ideas under serial might easily move into the realm of sequence. They could be developed by showing the scene and events from different viewpoints; that is, investigating the notion of space as well as time in relation to the chosen work.

The intention may be either to stimulate an emotion or thought, or to issue a directive. For example:

- The making of a dramative or narrative sequence which could range from a complex storyline, to the short but highly select images of a television commercial, or title sequence.
- Diagrams showing a process of abstraction or assemblage.
- A graphic design project might consist of finding ways in which to communicate a message without words e.g. how to tie a shoelace, make a pot of tea or operate a simple piece of machinery.

Some of Monet's late waterlily paintings and those of his Japanese bridge at Giverny may be considered as sequential works. Although more often than not called a series or serial some are, when considered

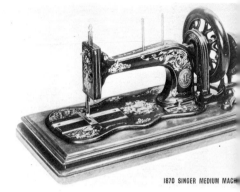

1870 SINGER MEDIUM MACH

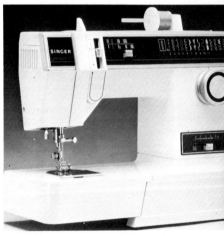

Above Singer sewing machines. Industrial design development

Top right Battle between the Assyrians and the Elamites. Section of a bas relief c. 660–650 BC from the South-West Palace, Nineveh. British Museum, London

Centre right The Miracles of St Zenobius. (From a series.) Sandro Botticelli. c. 1445–1510. National Gallery, London

Bottom right Pic Paper. Eunice Boothman. Photo story for less-able readers. 1980

Let me tell you about my visit to the fair. The fair was pitched on a common not too far from where my three girl friends lived.

We planned to meet there at 2 o'clock. I walked to the fair and waited by the big roundabout. My friends had not arrived yet.

I slipped onto one of the chairs and whizzed round very fast. That was fun, but it soon ended. I wished my friends were with me.

Then I saw them. They were waiting for a ride to start. I rushed over. I called and I waved. None of them waved back. They had not seen me.

Was I early or were they late I wondered? I looked at my watch. It seemed as if it had stopped.

So I stayed there. I hoped they would come soon. The roundabout filled and emptied and time passed.

Next moment they were carried up and away. Anger gripped me then. I hated them. They were having fun together and did not care about me.

As I backed away I hoped that no one saw that I had tears in my eyes. I didn't want to meet them now.

Six times the ride stopped and started. Why had they not bothered to meet me? I turned and moved away.

Well, I would enjoy the fair on my own. I mixed with the crowds looking for a ride to go on. There was such a lot to do.

My day was messed up. I felt that I was the only one at the fair alone. Everywhere I looked people were together.

Even the dog was cared for and ice-cream shared with him. I really did feel sorry for myself.

131

collectively, individual parts of a continuous sequence. Many paintings by Picasso or Bacon could also be viewed as part of a sequence rather than as isolated works.

Sequence implies movement

- Ancient sculpture e.g. Assyrian bas reliefs
- Trajan's column
- Greek pottery
- Medieval manuscripts
- Narrative paintings and contemporary advertising
- Flick books
- Early photographs with blurred figures
- Photographs by Muybridge
- Photographs by Marey
- Paintings by Marcel Duchamp e.g. *Nude Descending a Staircase* 1912
- Frames from movie films and videos
- Animated films

Sequence and time

Linear sequences consist of related images which tell a story in a logical time sequence, or explain a particular activity or mechanical function. Flash back and forward may be part of this.

There is a difference between real time and visual time which may be seen in cinema or television, related paintings or comic strips. Examples of condensed and extended time may be found in the films of Eisenstein, Flaherty, Antonioni, Renais, Godard and, in fact, probably most film and video makers. Rarely is real time used in media communication. The early films of Robert Flaherty, for example, *Nanook of the North* and Andy Warhol, for example, *Sleep*, are exceptions.

Sequence and visual narrative

Stories are sequences. In addition to written stories there are of course visual narratives, e.g. Trajan's Column, the Bayeaux Tapestry, *Marriage à la Mode* and *The Rake's Progress* by Hogarth, Indian temple sculpture, Assyrian bas reliefs, medieval manuscripts, drawings and paintings by David Hockney. There are also those images which communicate a narrative on a single picture plane. For example, *Adam and Eve in the Garden of Eden* by Pol de Limbourg, *Cupid and Psyche* by Jacopo del Sellaio and the paintings by Botticelli in the

Above Initial sketches for a sequence from the animated film, 'Henry's Cat Goes to Hollywood'. Bob Godfrey

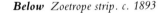

Below Zoetrope strip. c. 1893

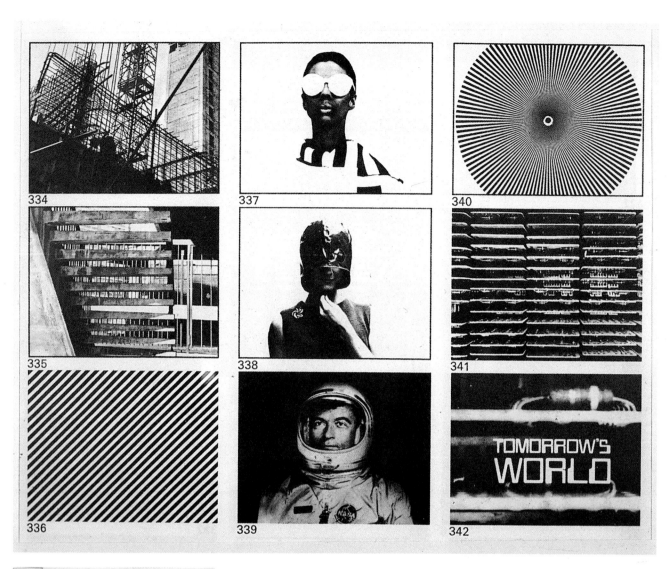

334
335
336
337
338
339
340
341
342

Top *Television graphics. Roy Laughton.*
Studio Vista

Above *Muslim instruction poster*

National Gallery, London of *Four Scenes from the Early Life of S. Zenobius*. The Spanish painter Genovés is also worth considering as a possible source of ideas for work on this theme.

Strip cartoons

- Victorian strip narratives e.g. Leech in Punch
- Cartoons in newspapers
- Cartoon strips in comics
- Strip sequences in advertising
- Strip sequences in painting e.g. Kitaij, Paolozzi, Hamilton
- Strip cartoons and the cinema e.g. Godard, Renais, Fellini
- Animated films

Sequence as non-narrative communication

- Television graphics e.g. Tomorrow's World
- Paintings by Hamilton, Paolozzi, Warhol, Degas
- Advertising
- Television pop videos
- Magazine layout and content juxtoposition
- Films
- Accidental sequence: magazine pages, newspaper, television programming, street posters

Metamorphosis. Kenneth Martin.
1974. Pen on paper. Each drawing
25.2 × 20.0 cm. The British Council

Movement and Time

Movement implies time. Aspects of this theme have been touched upon in the section dealing with projects on the theme series, serial and sequence. To a certain extent series of images, which may range from paintings or sculpture on one subject, to variations on a design problem, or related television programmes, represent the element of time, although they may not take that as the main consideration.

Above Amy, Wonderful Amy. *Joanna Buxton. Tapestry. Courtesy of the artist*

135

Serial and sequence, however, do by their very nature, deal with both movement and time. Perhaps the simplest introduction to the theme of movement and time would be to link it to the concept of series, serial and sequence. Relationships are apparent; only the parameters need to be defined by individual interests and requirements.

Movement and the problems of its representation have intrigued visual artists from the age when moving animals appeared on cave walls, to Futurism's simultaneous viewpoints, and the cross-cut montages of film and video. Between, there are many interpretations well known to teachers of art and design.

Movement may also be present in art and design in a non-representational way. Lines, shapes, forms and colours are arranged in patterns and rhythms, not to represent natural movement but to evoke feelings and emotions, responses to the idea of movement. This abstract interpretation has been utilised in the compositional devices and structural organisations of painters, sculptors and architects. We have only to analyse the use of diagonals and curves, and the deployment of forms and colour in art; tracery, fan vaulting and unit repitition in building, and the interweaving of architecture, sculpture and painting in so many ecclesiastical environments, to appreciate the way in which movement has been used to excite the emotions of the spectator. A concern for movement in art, craft and design may also be seen in the artefacts made in cultures and countries other than those influenced by the Western European tradition e.g. Islamic tiles and caligraphy.

Movement in Western European painting and sculpture has, until the late nineteenth and early twentieth century, usually been depicted as the instant moment of time caught and held in a single image. There are numerous examples of this which do not need identifying here. There are also, however, those images which show more than a single image and, in doing so, communicate some aspect of time as well as movement. For example (in addition to the pictures mentioned in the section on portraits), those paintings which depict a character at different stages of life or at different stages of a sequence of events, for example:

- *John the Baptist Retiring to the Desert* by Giovanni di Paolo (active 1420–82) National Gallery, London.

Top right Boxer with Yellow Shorts. Sam Rabin. *Wax crayon on board. 24.4 × 14.5 cm*
Bottom right Swimming doll, Bethnal Green Museum of Childhood
Left Cyclist. Kubatabahan Temple, Bali. Stone carving.

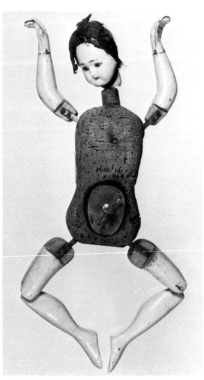

136

Fall and Expulsion from Paradise by Pol de Limbourg 15c. Musée Cluny, Paris.

Cupid and Psyche by Jacopo del Sellaio, Fitzwilliam Museum, Cambridge.

■ Paintings which contain on one picture-plane images of apparently the same person e.g. *Women Combing their Hair* by Edgar Degas (1875–6) Phillips Collection, Washington.

The sequential form of interpreting movement came into its own with the artist's appreciation of photography, film and the early

experiments of Etienne-Jules Marey and Eadweard Muybridge whose pioneering photographic work not only altered the accepted conventions of movement representation, but influenced the work of artists as different as Degas, Duchamp and Bacon.

Film-making, the related development of sequential photography, gave artists the medium for exploring not just logical time sequences, but the possibility of re-organising movement and time. Movement could become emphasised by repetition and dislocation, time could be real, condensed or extended – all devices which are evident in today's film and television programmes. Pop video is a form of the medium which uses such re-organisations of movement and time to a considerable degree. What we see today in such presentations would have been misunderstood and unacceptable in the early days of film and electronic communication. Re-organisations of movement and time are an integral part of the young person's everyday experience and it seems only sensible, and educationally appropriate, that as teachers we take them into account when planning our courses. Any consideration of movement and time should involve some element of film and photographic studies, which might well include video, as a practical component as well as an area for critical consideration. These media are available, are part of the language of art and design, are tools of the trade as much as they are part of everyone's leisure experience; and so as teachers we have a responsibility to utilise and consider them as part of the education process, as we should also become conversant with the new computer technology.

Above Toyota Advertisement with Muybridge photographs

138

Areas of study

- Movement and time in representational and non-representational art and design.
- The single image – a caught moment in time, e.g. Tiepolo, Gericault, Degas, Bacon.
- Related images:
  1 Separate pictures e.g. Hogarth;
  2 A number of images on one picture-plane e.g. Icons, Muybridge, photo stories, comic strips, Genovés.
- Multiple viewpoints:
  Architects' plans and elevations;
  Persian drawings;
  Cubist paintings indicating movement of the painter's and/or spectator's viewpoint;
  Futurist work e.g. Balla, Boccioni, Duchamp, Severini.

Above Fortitude and Wisdom. *Giovanni Tiepolo. 1743. Oil on canvas. 64.2 × 35.6 cm. Dulwich Picture Gallery, London.*

Right *Calendar – St Isidore. c. 1120. St John's College, Cambridge*

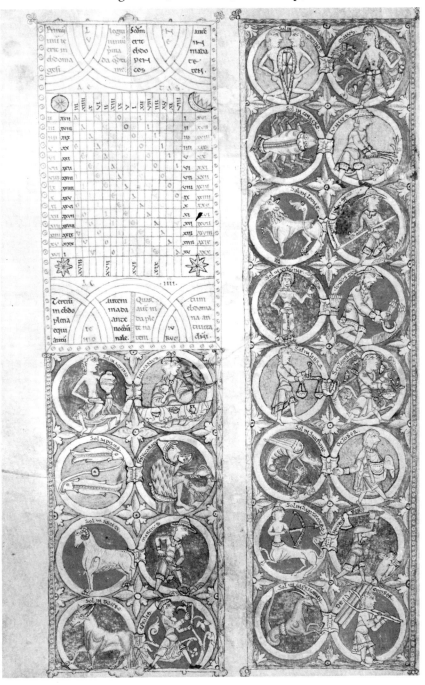

- Films with sequences of still shots e.g. *Le Jetée* – Chris Marker, *Battleship Potemkin* – Sergei Eisenstein.
- The relationships between shots in live action films.
- Camera movements related to the movement of actors, the setting and mood.
- Photographic interpretations of the theme e.g. blurred images.
- Non-representational images indicating the theme, particularly the movement aspect, can be found in much design and decoration, objects and architecture as well as in the obvious examples of paintings by Vasarely and Riley and the sculpture and mobiles of Calder, Tinguley and Martin.
- The way in which artists and designers use the elements of art to animate surface or take the eye moving into illusory depth, is also worth study.
- Movement and time related to nature: growth, water, wind, fire and earth, the seasons, the action of the human body e.g. gesture, dance, swimming and other sports, wind-powered and water-powered movement. Happenings and the 'assemblages' of such people as Gilbert and George. Links with dance, drama, mime, music and science are evident here.
- Movement and time related to man-made mechanisms (clocks, machines to generate power, to facilitate transport etc.) may be linked to kinetic art, light pictures, sculpture and computer graphics.
- Movement may imply time, but neither necessarily indicate progress or an advance. Disintegration and decay are as much a part of the theme as are flashbacks and time shifts, history and memory.

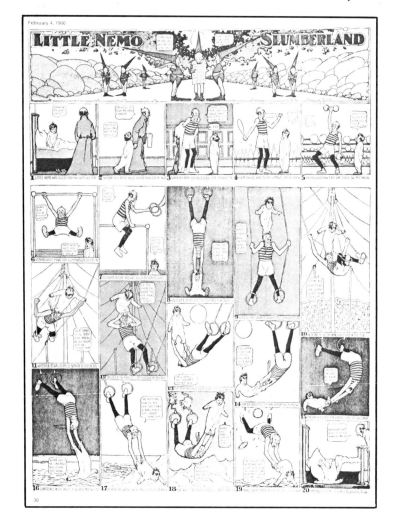

Top right Oriental calendar

Bottom right Dorothy Hodkin. *Maggi Hamling. 1985. National Portrait Gallery, London*

Left Little Nemo in Slumberland. *Windsor McCay. 4 February 1906*

Top left Ice Arch. *Brough, Cumbria, 1982. Andy Goldsworthy*

Top right Battle of Britain, August–October, 1940. *Paul Nash. Oil on canvas. 48 × 72 cm. Imperial War Museum, London*

Bottom right *Loie Fuller. Victorian engraving*

At Rest.

The Serpent Dance.

The Serpent Dance.

The Spiral.

SKIRT-DANCING.—MLLE. LOIE FULLER AND HER TRANSFORMATIONS.

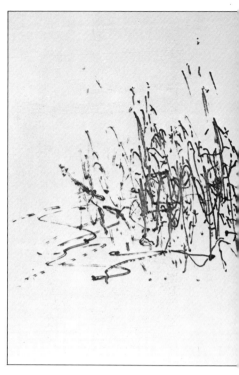

Top left *Clock*

Top right *Drawing made by a Tingley drawing machine. 1984. 30.5 × 25.4 cm. Collection Fanny Baldwin*

Bottom left *Computer Graphics. Amanda Andrew. 1987. A sequence showing the development of an image from a two-dimensional drawing to a three-dimensional form.*

Top right *Drawings from the Twin Elliptic Pendulum, a Victorian drawing machine.*

Bottom right Pheasant with its Head in Five Positions. *Tabriz. 1520–40. British Museum. London*

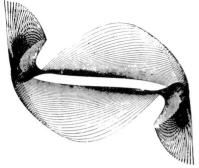

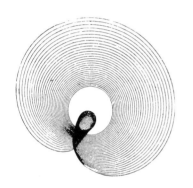

Conclusion

In conclusion it should be remembered that art and design education is not only about aquiring skills, learning about perception, teaching about context and encouraging expression and critical awareness. It is about all these, but it is also about providing the opportunity for the understanding of concepts and the formulating of opinions and ideas, enabling thinking and fostering a sense of wonder and curiosity which will enable students to make links and understand relationships in all they see.

To achieve this we must involve the students, allow for the guided development of their interests and ideas; devise schemes of work which are not so banal or abtruse as to alienate, yet whilst being within their experience demand an extension and provide for a sense of achievement. In addition it is important that critical and communication faculties, verbal as well as visual, should be learned and exercised for we are not in the business of training artists, but of educating people to be visually literate, sufficiently confident and erudite to express their thoughts and considered opinions on art and design and to make critical appraisal of the world around them.

Book List

Abbs, P. (ed.), *Living Powers: The Arts in Education*, Falmer Press, 1987.

Ames-Lewis, F., *Drawing in the Renaissance Workshop*, Victoria & Albert Museum, 1983.

Ashwin, C., *Encyclopaedia of Drawing*, Batsford, 1982.

Barrett, M., *Art Education: a Stategy for Course Design*, Heinemann, 1979.

Baynes, K., *About Design*, Design Council, 1976.

Cross, N. and Roy, R., *Design Methods Manual. Man-made Futures: Units 13–16*, Open University, 1975.

Dawson, J. (ed.), *Prints and Printmaking*, Phaidon, 1981.

Duberry, F. and Willats, J., *Drawing Systems*, Studio Vista, 1972.

Dyson, A., *Etching and Engraving: Technique and Tradition*, Longman, 1986.

Eirwen Jones, M., *A History of Western Embroidery*, Studio Vista, 1969.

Gernsheim, H. and A., *Creative Photography: Aesthetic Trends 1839 to Modern Times*, Bonanza Books, New York, 1962.

Gombrich, E., *The Story of Art*, Phaidon, 1950.

Gostelow, M. (ed.), *The Complete Guide to Needlework: Materials and Techniques*, Phaidon, 1982.

Green, P., *Design Education: Problem Solving and Visual Experience*, Batsford, 1974.

Hayter, S., *About Prints*, Oxford 1962.

Lowndes, D., *Film Making in Schools*, Batsford, 1968.

Moholy-Nagy, S., *Matrix of Man: an Illustrated History of the Urban Environment*, Pall Mall Press, 1968.

Palmer, F., *Visual Awareness*, Batsford, 1972.

Palmer, F., *Encyclopaedia of Oil Painting Materials and Techniques*, Batsford, 1984.

Pevsner, N., *The Englishness of English Art*, Architectural Press, 1956.

Pevsner, N., *Pioneers of Modern Design*, Pelican, 1974.

Piper, D., *Enjoying Paintings*, Pelican, 1964.

Read, H., *A Concise History of Modern Sculpture*, Thames and Hudson, 1964.

Read, H., *A Concise History of Modern Painting*, Thames and Hudson, 1974.

Robinson, K. (ed.), *The Arts in Schools – Principles, Practice and Provision*, The Gulbenkian Foundation, 1982.

Rowntree, D., *Assessing Students – How Shall We Know Them?* Harper and Rowe, 1977.

Scharf, A., *Creative Photography*, Studio Vista, 1965.

Scharf, A., *Art and Photography*, Pelican, 1974.

Storey, J., *Textile Printing*, Thames and Hudson, 1978.

Swann, Lord, *Education for All (The Swann Report)*, HMSO, 1985.

Taylor, R., *Educating for Art: Critical Response and Development*, Longman, 1986.

Thompson, D. (ed.), *Discrimination and Popular Culture*, Penguin, 1964.